Logical Answers to Life's Toughest Questions

The Rational Basis for Faith in Christ

Theological Insights of a Progressive Christian

by Richard H Goyette

Published by

Richard Goyette Enterprises

Phone: 530-588-5075

Email: richardinparadise@gmail.com

Website: www.ToughestLifeQuestions.com

Foreword

This book is the result of a life-long search for answers to questions that to one degree or another had prevented me from fully embracing a strong and uncompromising faith in Christ. As a young man I desperately wanted to fully believe in the Gospel of Christ, but was prevented from doing so because of major intellectual doubts. Over the years I continued to serve Christ to the best of my ability, but secretly I yearned for the kind of rock-solid unquestioning faith that I saw in others whose faith seemed to be much stronger than mine.

In the past, I regarded my intellect as a major hindrance to faith. I now realize that it was actually a gift from God. For a time, it prevented me from exercising strong faith in God. Eventually, however, my ability to apply sound logic and reason in my search for truth led to a much stronger faith than would otherwise have been possible.

An unquestioned faith, can start out strong, but often falters when assailed by the storms of life. When doubts arise, without satisfactory answers, negative emotions can overwhelm our efforts to stay the course in the face of adversity.

A questioning faith can grow stronger and stronger over time as we gradually find the answers. We are not likely to find many of those answers unless we first seek for them and diligently apply ourselves in our search for truth.

You probably wouldn't be reading this book if you were sure of all the answers. Congratulations! The first step in the pursuit of knowledge is asking the important questions. I hope you will be blessed by some of the answers I will be sharing with you.

Table of Contents

Prologue ....p. 9

The Rational Basis for Christian Faith

Chapter 1 ....p. 14

Questions that Bothered Me the Most

Chapter 2 ....p. 17

My Theology in a Nutshell

Chapter 3 ....p. 20

Is the Bible Literally True and/or Inerrant?

Chapter 4 ....p. 26

Reasons to Believe

Chapter 5 ....p. 33

Extra-Biblical Truths about God

Chapter 6 ....p. 47

Christian Salvation

Chapter 7 ....p. 56

The Atonement

Chapter 8 ....p. 65

The Trinity

Chapter 9 ....p. 73

Theological Correctness

Chapter 10 ....p. 82

Popular Misconceptions about Hell

Chapter 11 ....p. 95

Predestination and Free-Will

Chapter 12 .... p. 105

The Nature of Reality

Chapter 13 .... p. 115

Materialism, Dualism, and Idealism

Chapter 14 .... p. 120

NDE's, Reincarnation, and Christian Theology

Chapter 15 .... p. 126

Situational Ethics and the Law of Love

Chapter 16 .... p. 130

The King and the Crown Prince

Appendix .... p. 134

Leftovers from Richard's Table – *Additional Thoughts and Reflections*

P. 134 - **What Is Forgiveness, Really?**

P. 135 - **Entering the Kingdom and the Law of Sowing and Reaping**

P. 137 - **What Happens when We Turn to a Different Gospel?**

P. 138 - **Inch by Inch, Anything's a Cinch.**

P. 139 - **You Can Catch More Flies with Honey than with Vinegar.**

P. 140 - **Separating the Sheep from the Goats**

P. 140 - **Wisdom Should Not Be Equated with Certitude.**

P. 141 - **The Best reward for Doing Good**

P. 142 - **Is God the Author of Sin and Evil?**

P. 143 - **What about Hitler?**

P. 143 - **The key to Successful Christian Living**

P. 144 - **Why Atheists Hate Christianity**

P. 144 - **My View of Bible Inspiration**

P. 145 - **The Moral Dilemma of Compartmentalization**

P. 146 - **God's Self-Adjusting Universe**

P. 146 - **Little Things Can Make a Big Difference.**

P. 147 - **The Goal of Christian Missions**

P. 148 - **Happiness Comes from Within.**

P. 149 - **Sin Is Our Enemy, Not God.**

P. 150 - **La La Land or Law Law Land**

P. 151 - **How to Get the Dirty Bone out of Your Dog's Mouth**

P. 152 - **Believers Will Enter the Kingdom Ahead of Unbelievers.**

P. 153 - **The Pearl of Great Price**

P. 154 - **The God Within**

P. 155 - **The Parable of the Persistent Widow**

P. 157 - **Like Father Like Son**

P. 158 - **The Four Spiritual Laws**

P. 160 - **Taking Hold of God**

P. 161 - He Was There All the Time.

P. 162 - A Broken Body Can Only Be Healed by Reattaching the Severed Members.

P. 163 - It's the Living that's Important, Not the Understanding

P. 164 - What Is Meant by the Resurrection of the Body?

P. 165 - Here's a Real Mind-Bender for You.

P. 167 - The Water Is Calm Beneath the Surface.

P. 168 - The Sick and Dying Don't Need More Bad News.

P. 169 - God's Lost & Found

P. 170 - Does Satan Really Exist?

P. 171 - What Is a Christian?

P. 172 - We Are Saved by Grace.

P. 173 - What Should We Be Praying For?

P. 174 - The Greatest Commandment

P. 176 - The Cancellation of Our Sin Debt

P. 178 - How to Experience a Personal Relationship with God

P. 178 - The Fatherhood of God

Prologue

The Rational Basis for Christian Faith

People embrace the Christian faith for a variety of reasons. Most of us, however, including myself, became Christians through a process of cultural indoctrination. We were raised in Christian homes and became Christians because we wanted to be Christians. We wanted to please our parents and we enjoyed the sense of belonging that comes with membership in a Christian group. A variety of emotions and motives were involved. Some of us were attracted to the warmth and love we received from our Christian brothers and sisters, and we enjoyed the security of the group membership. We also enjoyed the sense of privilege that comes with belonging to an exclusive organization. And, of course, we all want to go to Heaven when we die. Who wouldn't? Basically, we embraced Christianity because we wanted to be Christians for emotional, rather than intellectual reasons.

The rational basis for our faith tends to be subjective, rather than deductive in nature. Through a process of highly subjective reasoning we seek validation for our belief system, rather than arriving at our belief system through an objective process of logical deduction. We like to think that there is a strong, rational basis for our beliefs, but the truth is, we believe mostly because we want to believe. For most of us, Christian apologetics (defending the faith) takes the form of a highly selective process of evaluation, when studying the evidence. If the findings of science conflict with the Bible, rather than alter the way we interpret the Bible, we alter our interpretation of the scientific data. When confronted with a logical inconsistency within our theological belief system, rather than seeking a resolution to the problem, we live with the contradiction and call it a paradox, instead.

For people like us, the prospect of starting from scratch, as it were, and objectively examining all the evidence is almost unthinkable. It would be tantamount to abandoning our faith without any assurance that our investigation would yield a happy result. Because of this, all our well-intentioned theological and scientific investigations are tinged by faith-colored glasses. In all honesty, as much as I would like to think that my theological investigations over the years have been impartial, and my conclusions based on pure deductive reasoning, that is simply not the case. It is impossible to completely remove from one's mind all presuppositions prior to embarking on a quest for truth.

I will say this, however. Because I am basically analytical and rational by nature, rather than intuitive and emotional, the process was a bit easier for me. My faith was never rock solid to begin with. It was full of intellectual holes that I could not fill. I was plagued by many serious doubts. When I began a serious process of investigation about ten years ago, it was easier for me to at least temporarily let go of many sacred cows in my belief system for the sake of objectivity. I earnestly prayed every day for God to lead me to the truth, no matter where it led.

Our emotional attachment to our faith is a two-edged sword. On the positive side, we enjoy the comfort and security of an unquestioned faith. On the negative side, there are many unpleasant aspects of that faith that we must live with. For my efforts, I was rewarded with the comfort and security of a revised faith, without the nagging doubts and contradictions. My view of God has been greatly expanded, and I have a renewed appreciation for the scope and extent of God's love.

Recognizing and admitting contradictions in our current belief system is how we grow morally, ethically, and spiritually. If you feel that your beliefs do not have to be "logical" in order to be true, why do you believe that? What arguments would you present to prove that logic is not necessary? All belief systems have at their root basic logical assumptions, even religious beliefs. "Blind faith" is not really blind at all. It is a decision one makes, with eyes wide open, to accept someone else's belief system, rather than one's own, without necessarily understanding the logic behind it or the underlying premises on which it is based. Why would any rational person want to become a Christian if there are no good "reasons" to do so? Sadly, most people cling to illogical and harmful belief systems mainly due to emotional dependence and fear. Reason, common sense, and logic should lie at the foundation of your religious belief system. My faith in the Gospel of Christ is stronger today than it was years ago, mainly because it is no longer illogical and self-contradictory. According to the Bible, perfect love casts out fear, and God is love. If you can believe that, then you don't need to be afraid to ask the tough questions. Don't be afraid of the answers you might find. All truth is God's truth. Jesus is the way, the TRUTH, and the life. If God is love, He will continue to love you, no matter what.

Hebrews 11:1 *"Now faith is the assurance of things hoped for, the conviction of things not seen."*

Faith is not a prerequisite for salvation; it is simply the means by which God enables us to experience it. We can't see God, Heaven, or the Age to come. During our earthly walk, we can experience them only by faith. We cannot see God's love. We cannot see the mind of God or His emotions and attitudes towards us. Jesus said that the experience of being born of God is like feeling the wind. You cannot see it, but you know it is there by its affects. When you unfurl the sail of faith, you tap into and are carried along by it. God's unconditional love and acceptance of all of us, is like that wind. It is there for everyone. It already belongs to everyone. The wind is not turned on or off by our belief in its existence. In order to experience its effect on us, what I would call Christian salvation, we need to raise the sail of faith.

When I was young, I was unsure of my salvation, because I wasn't able to muster up what I believed was the necessary amount of faith. No matter how hard I tried, I could not rid myself of intellectual doubts about God's existence and the inerrancy of the Scriptures. I had trouble fully embracing the apparently

11

exclusionary doctrine of salvation by faith in Christ alone. I had trouble believing that a supposedly loving God would send people to endless torment in Hell, simply for not believing the correct religious doctrines. Despite my doubts, I was drawn to the positive aspects of the Gospel, so I confessed Christ as Savior and Lord anyway, hoping that one day I would be able to muster up the kind of faith that seemed evident in the lives of other believers whom I envied. I wished with all my heart that I could have the same kind of unquestioning faith that they had. I felt that I was somehow cursed with a questioning intellect that prevented me from exercising complete faith in God.

Eventually, God rewarded my efforts, as I came to the understanding that the strength of my faith was not nearly as important as the strength and trustworthiness of the One in whom I had placed my faith. As I hoisted my feeble sail of faith, the winds of God's Holy Spirit did in fact take hold. As time went by, I was able to let out more and more sail, as God revealed more of His truths to me. Eventually, as I discarded many false beliefs about God and substituted more of the truth, I found myself being carried along not just by an occasional breeze, but by the higher and much stronger trade winds. Instead of muddling along in a little dingy, I now feel like the captain of a mighty clipper ship.

If you at times find yourself floundering on the rocks of confusion and doubt, please don't despair. If you don't believe anything else about God, just try and believe this. God is love. He is all powerful. He is omnipresent. He loves everyone, including you. Like the wind, He is there for everyone. If you sincerely desire to experience the love of God, put up your little sail of faith and do the best you can to live your life according to the teachings of Christ. Don't be afraid to ask all those good questions, and God will provide you with the answers you need. As you exercise the little bit of faith that you already possess God will multiply your efforts, and the size of your sail will grow. Don't worry about all the negative stuff. For now, just immerse yourself in the good stuff, the love of God.

Please do your best to read this book with an open mind, as difficult as that is to do. The worst that can happen is that you reject my arguments and settle back into your comfort zone. The best that can happen is that you will discover some very satisfying and believable answers to questions that up until now may have been a hindrance to your faith.

Chapter 1

Questions that Bothered Me the Most

When I was young, I could never be sure that I was a genuine "born-again" Christian, mainly because I wasn't ever given satisfactory answers to many perplexing questions. Nevertheless, I did profess faith in Christ from a very early age, and throughout my life I have been actively engaged in church activities. I did my best to live my faith, despite serious doubts and reservations. It was not until very late in my life that I have been able to answer all of those questions with complete confidence and intellectual honesty.

Here is a list of questions that bothered me the most. As you read these questions, ask yourself how you would answer each of them. Are you completely satisfied with your answers? Are there questions on the list for which you have no satisfactory answer?

1. How can I know for absolute sure that God exists?

2. If God does exist, why does He hide Himself from us? Why does He make it so difficult for us to believe in Him? Why doesn't He just visibly show Himself to all of us, thereby removing all doubts about His existence? If unbelievers will be condemned to everlasting Hell when they die, why wouldn't God make it easier for them to believe?

3. If the Bible is truly God's word, why does it contain so many historical, scientific, and theological contradictions and inaccuracies? If all the words of Scripture are not inerrant and infallible, in what ways might they still reveal truths about God that can absolutely be relied upon?

4. Why would an all-powerful God of love condemn the majority of the human race to eternal torture in Hell? Why would God

command us to forgive our enemies and at the same time refuse to do so Himself?

5. If Christ paid the penalty on Calvary for the sins of mankind, why is most of humanity still required to pay the penalty? Either the penalty was paid or it wasn't, right?

6. If the penalty for sin is eternal torture in Hell, how could Christ have possibly paid that penalty on our behalf on Calvary? He wasn't eternally tortured in Hell. According to the Bible, He only remained in the grave for three days, and while there, he was not being tortured. Instead, He was preaching.

7. If belief or faith in Christ is necessary for salvation, how is a person to know what level of belief is required? For most Christians, belief is not absolute. It can only be measured in degrees. Some believe strongly, while others still harbor many doubts. How many doubts are permissible? How strong does one's belief need to be? Where does God draw the line between saving faith and faith that doesn't quite cut it?

8. If repentance from sin is necessary for salvation, how complete does that repentance need to be? Most of us continue to sin, despite being sorry for our sins. Is there any way to know for sure that we have adequately repented of the sin in our lives? Where does God draw the line?

9. Why is Christian salvation an all-or-nothing proposition, either eternal bliss in Heaven or eternal misery in Hell? Wouldn't it be more fair and just for God to impose rewards and punishments in an equitable and proportionate fashion?

10. Both Calvinists and Arminians believe that people are helpless to save themselves, and the intervention of the Holy Spirit is required to bring sinners to repentance. Why is it that the Holy Spirit does not intervene on everyone's behalf to change their hearts and draw them back to God?

11. Most people who reject Christianity do so because of strong cultural biases and non-Christian religious indoctrination, usually from a very early age. Can these people really be blamed

for their lack of faith in Christ? Is it fair that God would condemn them all to eternal Hell merely for being a product of their culture and upbringing?

12. What are we to make of God-approved genocide in the Bible? Examples include the Genesis flood, the killing of all the first-born of Egypt prior to the Exodus, the subsequent conquest of Canaan, and God's continuing support of Israel in various wars against her enemies.

13. If only Christians go to Heaven when they die, why is it that both Christian and non-Christian near death experiencers (even atheists) have similar experiences while in Heaven? If the near death experience is a demonic deception, why is it that both Christians and non-Christians experience the same deception?

14. Why does God not intervene to alleviate human suffering and evil in this world?

If you were to ask these questions to your pastor, he or she would undoubtedly offer a pat answer to each of them. By now, most of you have heard those answers. The question I would ask you is this. How satisfied are you with those answers? For me, those pat answers were very unsatisfying. Today, I can honestly say that I have arrived at answers that not only resolve all the contradictions and paradoxes of popular Christianity, but I have been able to do it without having to throw my brains out the window. I am no longer forced to live with logical incongruities. The basic tenets of my faith are not only supported by the spirit and intent of the Christian Scriptures, but also by other sources of truth, including non-Christian religious experience, science, intuition, reason, logic, and common sense.

Chapter 2

My Theology in a Nutshell

Over the past 10 years or so my theology has undergone a huge metamorphosis. I re-explored the Christian Scriptures with an open mind and a fresh set of eyes. In addition, I have read extensively on the subjects of theology, life after death, the nature of reality, quantum physics, near death experiences, mysticism, out-of-body experiences, and the like. I searched for truth wherever it might be found. I began my search with the premise that truth is truth, and all truth must be God's truth, no matter where one finds it. When I began my search I regarded myself to be an evangelical Christian, neither fundamentalist, nor liberal, but somewhere in between. I subscribed to the orthodox tenets of the Christian faith, but had serious reservations about many doctrines which seemed contradictory or paradoxical in nature, especially doctrines relating to salvation and eternal hell.

During this process, my concepts of God and the nature of reality have changed, as well as my beliefs regarding the atonement, the nature and purpose of God's judgments, the nature of the afterlife, and the purpose of our earthly existence. I now believe that we are eternally existing spiritual beings temporarily residing in quasi-physical bodies. I believe that the Christian and Hebrew Scriptures are a historical record of mankind's evolving and improving ideas about the nature of God and how He relates to us. I believe they are inspired by God and full of God's truth, but they are definitely not infallible and inerrant. I believe that recent discoveries in science, parapsychology, the nature of reality, and life after death are supported by the Scriptures, especially the teachings of Jesus Christ and the Apostle Paul. I now consider myself to be a "progressive" Christian, as opposed to a conservative or evangelical Christian. I no longer believe that Christian salvation is mostly about who goes to Heaven or Hell when they die. Instead, I believe it refers to an ages-long process of becoming like Christ. We are all on that path.

I believe that God is love and God loves us all unconditionally. I believe that we are all children of God, made in God's spiritual likeness, and we all share the divine nature. I believe that we all reap what we sow, both Christians and non-Christians alike, the purpose of which is to teach us important life lessons and help us to grow spiritually. I believe the purpose of our existence here on earth, and also in the heavenly realms, is to enjoy life, help others to do the same, and in the process become more like Christ. I believe that Heaven and Hell are not places, but states of being. I believe that the separation we feel from God and others is an illusion. God is always with us, and we are all connected with each other and with God, more intimately than most of us realize. I believe that theological correctness has nothing at all to do with our standing with God, and that not having all the answers is part of God's plan for us and serves a very useful purpose. I believe that "getting saved" is not an instantaneous event. It is an ages-long process of becoming consciously aware of God's presence in our lives and acting it out with deeds of kindness and generosity. Loving our neighbors as ourselves is exactly the same as loving God.

My purpose in writing this book is to offer help to those of you who have unanswered questions about your faith and are looking for answers that line up solidly not only with the spirit and intent of the Christian Scriptures but also with the findings of science and other non-Biblical sources of truth. This book is for the person who is looking for theological truth that conforms squarely with sound reason and logic. It is for the person who is hungry for spiritual truth that can be believed and lived wholeheartedly, without the doubts and reservations that often accompany traditional belief systems.

A lot of what you read in this book will surprise you. I will be sharing some concepts that may be entirely new to you, especially if you have not ventured outside of evangelical Christian circles.

There are millions of people out there who largely share my views. Many of these people you will find in progressive Christian churches. A lot of them will never set foot inside a church for a variety of good and not-so-good reasons. Some of them will be found among adherents to non-Christian religions.

Many of you will be shocked by what you find in the Scriptures that you never noticed before. Important truths in Scripture are sometimes completely missed because people tend to read into the Scriptures what they have heard from the pulpits and in Sunday school classes. When you take off your "theologically tinted" glasses and seek honest and unbiased ways of looking at and interpreting the Bible, many passages will take on completely different meanings. Some of them will take on meanings that are exactly opposite of what you previously believed them to mean.

The result of my personal quest for truth was better than I could ever have imagined. My faith is now rock-solid, and I am more excited than ever about where I am headed in this life and the next. If you are honestly seeking answers to life's toughest questions and aren't afraid of the truth, wherever it leads, get ready for the ride of your life.

Chapter 3

Is the Bible Literally True and/or Inerrant

There is a difference between literal truth and inerrancy. The Bible may be considered inerrant, while at the same time make use of symbolic imagery and metaphors for purposes of illustration. The question of inerrancy has more to do with theological, scientific, and historical truth. So, a better way to rephrase the title of this chapter might be this. Is the Bible the inerrant word of God? Or is it the God-inspired words of fallible men, and not true and inerrant in every respect? If the Bible is not completely inerrant, does this negate the parts that are true? If not, how does one decide which parts to believe and which parts to reject? Orthodox Christians can be sharply divided on this issue, while at the same time sharing similar "theological" beliefs and subscribing to nearly identical doctrinal statements and creeds.

Here's my take on this issue. In the pages of the Bible you will find totally reliable information regarding the true character of God and how you may establish a relationship with Him. Please understand, however, that not even the most hard-core Christian fundamentalist believes that every Bible passage is literally true. Some passages are obviously figurative in nature. For example, in Psalm 96:12 we learn that when the Lord comes to judge the earth all the trees of the forest will sing for joy. Most of the parables of Jesus were fictional stories which illustrate spiritual truths. The apocalyptic passages in Daniel, Ezekiel, Revelation, and so on, speak of future events in symbolic terms. Up to this point, proponents of both sides of the inerrancy issue would be in agreement. Beyond this point, however, the issues become clouded.

The issue of inerrancy is complicated by the fact that many of the truths expressed in the Bible are understood, even by proponents of inerrancy, as being generally true, but not in every specific instance. For example, in Ephesians 6:2 children are admonished to honor their fathers and mothers so that everything will go well with them and that they may enjoy long life on the earth. In Proverbs 22:6, we are admonished to *"train a child in the way he should go, and when he is old he will not turn from it."* Obviously, not all obedient children live long lives and not all children who are raised in devoutly Christian homes make the right choices later in life.

Another related issue is the difficulty of separating the words of God from the words of man in the Scriptures. The writers of the Bible, although inspired by God, still expressed their own points of view, which were often contrary to God's truth. The entire books of Job and Ecclesiastes are illustrative of this. Job was under the mistaken notion that God always rewards the righteous and punishes the wicked in this life, and he was unable to understand why he was being punished. His friends were no help. They insisted that Job had committed some grievous sin and was justly suffering God's wrath. Despite all the give and take between Job and his friends, the issue was never clearly resolved. In the end, Job resigned himself to the fact that he should honor God despite, in his opinion, being unfairly treated. Eventually his health and possessions were restored, but one gets the feeling that this ending was added to satisfy those who could not accept the fact that life is not always fair. Was Job an actual historical character, or was the book intended to be understood as a parable illustrating man's inability to understand the ways of God?

In the case of Ecclesiastes, the writer begins with these words, *"Meaningless! Meaningless!"* says the teacher. *"Utterly meaningless! Everything is meaningless."* He goes on to explain how futile life is because, in the end (see Eccl. Chap. 9) all share a common destiny—*"the righteous and the wicked, the good and the bad, the clean and the unclean, those who offer sacrifices and those who do not . . . For the living know that they will die, but the dead know nothing; they have no further reward, and even the memory of them is forgotten."*

Although Jesus had great respect for the Scriptures, he also took liberties when interpreting them and rendered many of their teachings obsolete by supplanting them with newer doctrines. In Matthew 5, the Sermon on the Mount, Jesus emphasized the importance of the Law and the Prophets, and told us that *"until heaven and earth disappear, not the smallest letter, not the least stroke of a pen, will by any means disappear from the Law until everything is accomplished,"* and warned us not to break even the least of these commandments. However, He then went on to amplify and change six of these commandments. In the cases of murder, adultery, divorce, oaths, revenge, and hatred of enemies, he made the rules much stricter. Even strict Biblical literalists understand that individual Scriptures must be interpreted in light of the historical context in which they were given. In Old Testament times, due to the "hardness of peoples' hearts," God's laws were more lenient than the standards which he now holds us to.

I personally have come to believe that God's revelations to us through the inspired writers of the Bible are progressive in nature. Over time God has progressively revealed more of his truth. The fact that Solomon and Job were ignorant of an afterlife does not mean that their written works were not inspired by God. They were truthfully expressing what God had revealed to them. If we insist that all Scriptures are inerrant we fail to take into account the progressive nature of God's revelation. The writers of the Bible wrote in different historical contexts and with different purposes in mind. They were inspired by God, but they were not perfect, and their knowledge of spiritual and historical truths was not perfect.

For the most part, our view of God today is quite different from that of the ancient Hebrews. The religious and cultural identity of the Hebrews and, by extension, many modern day Christians, is deeply rooted in ancient stories and legends, many of which were borrowed from neighboring cultures, which were verbally passed down from one generation to the next. Many of those stories found their way into the Hebrew Scriptures. In my view, those stories do not have to be literally true in order to convey spiritual truth. In many of those stories, however, we sometimes see a very primitive view of God. For example, in the Garden of Eden God is pictured as physically walking around looking for Adam, and Satan is pictured as a talking serpent. I personally believe that it would be a serious mistake to base Christian doctrine on a literal interpretation of those stories. What I try to do when assigning meaning to those stories and traditions is to identify the progression of thought. In the Hebrew Bible we don't find literal Christian truth, but instead the origins of that truth. Valuable lessons are often learned through a process of trial and error, and this is evident in the lessons learned by the Nation of Israel and the Christian Church throughout history, as recorded in the Scriptures. In the life and teachings of Jesus Christ, we see a culmination of this process. I do believe that God continues to reveal new truths to us today.

It is unsettling for most of us to realize that the particular religious doctrines that form the basis of our purpose in life, including our final destiny after death, are based on an imperfect document. It is helpful for me to understand that our view of perfection may not be the same as God's. A pitcher does not have to be perfectly shaped, and free from surface cracks, to be perfectly suited for holding water. It apparently suits God to accomplish His goals for mankind through imperfect human intermediaries. He does almost nothing directly. We have been given the privilege of being used by God to accomplish His purposes, despite our weakness and imperfections.

Please understand that whether you believe in Scriptural inerrancy or not the fact remains that the Bible must be interpreted by examining a particular verse or passage in light of the historical context in which it was written, and other Scriptures dealing directly or indirectly with the same topic must also be examined. Any given Scripture, no matter how clear the interpretation may seem at first glance, is subject to a variety of interpretations. It may be regarded as figurative or symbolic in nature; it may be regarded as applying only to a particular period in Biblical history, only to be supplanted with other commands given at a later date; it may be regarded as the opinion of the writer, but not necessarily the words of God Himself, and so on. Individual verses and passages of Scripture must be viewed and interpreted in light of the totality of the Scriptures. The teachings of the New Testament shed light on the meaning and intended purpose of various passages in the Old Testament. In some cases the teachings of Christ supplant Old Testament teachings. In other cases New Testament teachings reveal hidden meanings in various Old Testament passages. In most cases, when faced with multiple possible interpretations of a given Bible passage, the intended meaning becomes clear only when other passages are examined which deal with the same topic.

For example, in Matthew 17, Jesus took his disciples aside and admonished them for their lack of faith. He told them that if they had faith even as small as a mustard seed they could move a mountain from here to there and nothing would be impossible to them. Other passages imply that we can have whatever we ask in Jesus' name, and so on (See Matt. 21:22; Jn. 16:24; Mk. 11:24). One could take a "literal" view of these passages and assume that if we just have enough faith we can get from God whatever we want. When other Bible passages are examined, however, we realize that "getting what we want" is not what prayer is all about. James tells us (4:3) that we don't get what we ask for because we ask with the wrong motives and pray selfishly. James also tells us (5:16) that the prayer of a righteous man is powerful and effective. Righteousness results from abiding in Christ and conforming our wills to His. When we are able to share the mind of Christ in this way, then what we want will be the same as what God wants and our prayers will indeed become very powerful. A guaranteed "yes" answer to prayer is not simply a matter of asking for whatever you may want at any given moment. When Jesus prayed in Gethsemane, He did not get what He wanted. He did get what He prayed for, however, because His prayer ended with these words, *"not my will, but thine be done."*

A very difficult issue for me personally to resolve was how far I could safely depart from the popular view of Scriptural inerrancy and still maintain my confidence in the Bible as a reliable source of

24

spiritual truth. Today I am able to accept most of the findings of "historical criticism" of the Bible, including source criticism, form criticism, redaction criticism, tradition criticism, canonical criticism, and so on, and still maintain my faith in the Gospel of Christ. Because my study of the Bible is not restricted or confined to a rigid view of inerrancy I am able to more honestly and accurately assess the development of thought throughout Bible history, as God has progressively revealed His truths to us. There is not space in this book to provide an exhaustive treatment of this subject. My main purpose in writing this chapter is to give you a basic understanding of my views regarding Bible inspiration and inerrancy. In subsequent chapters I will be providing Scriptural support for my views on a variety of topics. The ways in which I use Scripture to support those views will amply illustrate how I deal with the questions of inerrancy and progressive revelation when interpreting the Bible and uncovering underlying foundational truths about God and the Gospel of Christ.

I believe the best way to understand and interpret the Bible is to approach it with attitude of submission to Jesus Christ as the Lord of one's life. He is God's living Word to us. As you read the words of the Bible, which have come to you through the imperfect filter of human understanding and experience, trust Jesus Christ, who is Himself perfect, to guide you by His Holy Spirit.

I would like to mention at this point that the main theological positions I have taken in this book are totally supported by the Scriptures, no matter which view of inspiration one might hold. Many inerrantists, who disagree with my views regarding the inerrancy of the Scriptures, nevertheless strongly agree with my belief in the doctrine of universal reconciliation.

Chapter 4

Reasons to Believe

If you are like most people, you have struggled with the question of God's existence and more specifically the truth of the Bible. The purpose of this chapter is to help you understand why I believe in the God of the Bible, and in so doing help you to believe as well.

One of the main reasons many people do not believe in God is that God seems to operate behind the scenes. He hides Himself from us, and does not seem to answer our prayers. Imagine, for a minute what life might be like if God did visibly appear to all of us and we could see Him watching over everything we do, even things we do in secret. Now, further imagine what it would be like if God brought down the hammer and immediately whacked us on the side of the head every time we violated one of His rules or even entertained an unwholesome thought. Further imagine what it would be like if God were to instantly reward every good thought and action with a tangible reward. If that were the case, then our primary motivation for being good would be self-interest. We would be like Pavlov's dogs, who's responses were conditioned solely by external stimuli. Selfless, self-sacrificing *Agape* love could not exist in such an environment.

Another reason people find it hard to believe in God is related to the above. They cannot understand why a loving and powerful God would allow so much sin, suffering and evil to exist. The freedom that God gives us to make our own choices in life, without direct coercion from above, is like a two-sided coin. One side of the coin would represent the negative experiences of life, with the other side of the coin representing the positive experiences that would not be possible if those negative experiences did not exist. Negative experiences help us in two ways.

First they provide a backdrop which enables us to see and appreciate the positive. For example, light is accentuated by darkness. Love is most appreciated when one is most in need of it. The greater the offense, the greater the impact of a pardon. The greater the hurt, the more soothing the relief. The greater the sorrow, the greater the joy when the sorrow ends. Every single positive feeling or emotion is made possible and enhanced by the existence of its opposite.

The second way negative experiences help us is by the lessons learned. We cannot learn patience without trials. We cannot give sacrificially without sacrifice. We cannot learn to forgive if there are no offenses. The Apostle Paul said it like this in Romans 5:20, *"The law was brought in so that the trespass might increase. But where sin increased, grace increased all the more."* In another place, He said, *"For God has bound everyone over to disobedience so that he may have mercy on them all"* (Rom. 11:32). Selfless, self-sacrificing *Agape* love could not exist in world that is free from sin, suffering and evil.

So far, I have attempted to remove a couple of obstacles to belief in God. Now I would like to turn your attention to some reasons to believe. Please keep in mind that I will not be presenting irrefutable proofs of God's existence. For me, however, the evidence is so strong as to leave no room for reasonable doubt.

The best evidence of the existence of God, in my view, results from a process of "deductive" reasoning whereby conclusions are deduced from universally accepted scientific facts and historical truths. An example of this kind of reasoning would be calculating the probability of certain natural processes occurring without divine, supernatural intervention. According to Dr. Hugh Ross, a highly respected astrophysicist and pastor, the mathematical probability of even one planet existing in the universe which is capable of supporting life is much less than one chance in a hundred thousand trillion, trillion, trillion, trillion, trillion. A probability that small is for all practical purposes zero. Dr. Ross lists 75 criteria that must be satisfied for a planet to be capable of supporting life. He then calculates the probability of each of those criteria of existing in any one planet. If just one of those 75 criteria were not satisfied, then life would be impossible. When you multiply the 75 individual probabilities, you arrive at the probability of a planet existing that could support life. You will find these 75 criteria listed, along with their respective probability factors, on Dr. Ross' website www.reasons.org.

Using simple mathematical formulas, probabilities can also be calculated for other natural processes occurring without divine intervention, such as the creation of life on this planet or its evolution into higher forms. These probabilities are so infinitesimally small that they are basically zero. It would logically follow then, that the probability of the intelligent design of our universe, the planet Earth, and life on Earth, is infinitely great and for all practical purposes certain.

Additional scientific evidence for the existence of God may be found in the study of quantum mechanics and general relativity. Many scientists, especially theoretical physicists, are coming to realize that we don't actually live in a physical, material world, but a supernatural world instead. Their belief in a natural world, subject only to the natural laws of Newtonian physics, has given way the idea that the world we observe and experience consists solely of immaterial waves that may be described only as probabilities and possibilities, and do not "collapse" into reality unless observed by conscious observers. This lends support to the idea that we are, in a manner of speaking, spiritual, rather than physical beings. Later in this book this subject will be explored in greater detail. Belief in the supernatural makes it much easier for me to believe in a supernatural, immaterial, creator God.

The testimony of people who have experienced near death experiences (NDE's) provides strong evidence that God exists, and also gives us valuable insights into the reality of an afterlife in Heaven. The evidence for the reality and genuineness of these experiences is in my view irrefutable, and will be covered in more detail in a later chapter of this book.

Various polls have revealed that the vast majority of people on earth share my belief in the existence of God, but most do not believe in the divine inspiration of the Christian Scriptures. And that brings us to the second part of this chapter. Are the Christian Scriptures divinely inspired by God, and do we find within their pages reliable information about God's nature and how we may relate to Him.

My belief in the truth of the Christian Bible has been reinforced throughout my life by my own experiences of God working in my life and the lives of those around me, but the foundation of my belief includes both scientific and historical evidence. A powerful case for the truth of the Christian Scriptures can be made from historical evidence. In a court of law the guilt or innocence of the person on trial is supported by historical evidence. Known historical facts are corroborated by eye witnesses to "prove" the case. In the case of the Scriptures, there are many historical events which are universally accepted even by skeptics. We know that most of the original apostles, and many of their closest followers, suffered intense persecution and martyrdom for what they believed to be the truth of the resurrection, of which they were actual eye witnesses. It is much easier for me to believe the truth of their claims than to believe that they deliberately lied about it for personal advantage.

While I don't believe in the inerrancy of the Christian Scriptures, I do believe they were divinely inspired. Much of the Bible consists of stories, legends, sayings, and actual historical events that were handed down verbally for many years, and in some cases centuries, before they were written down. Even after taking written form they were subject to later additions and embellishments by well-meaning redactionists who exercised a form of poetic license with respect to the literal truth, in order to teach theological truths from their unique perspectives in history. This in my view doesn't make the Scriptures less true from a theological standpoint. It does, however, create problems when we base certain aspects of our theology on a literal interpretation of passages which might not be accurate in the objective historical sense.

For example, It may well be that the writers and editors of the Genesis accounts believed that the creation of the cosmos, including all mankind, occurred over a period of six literal 24-hour days. It is not necessary for us today to believe this in order to accept the underlying truth that God is, after all, still the creator of everything. At the same time, I would be careful not to develop a doctrine of original sin and/or the moral and spiritual depravity of mankind solely on a literal interpretation of the Genesis account, or to blame everything on Satan, who took the form of a serpent in the mythical Garden of Eden.

Another historical argument for the truth of the Scriptures, and the New Testament in particular, would be that there is no other good explanation for the influence of Christianity on subsequent human history. The following is an adaptation taken from a sermon by Dr. James Allan Francis in "The Real Jesus and Other Sermons," c. 1926, by the Judson Press of Philadelphia (pp 123-124 titled "Arise Sir Knight!"):

One Solitary Life

Here is a man who was born in an obscure village, the child of a peasant woman. He grew up in another village. He worked in a carpenter shop until He was thirty. Then for three years He was an itinerant preacher.

He never owned a home. He never wrote a book. He never held an office. He never had a family. He never went to college. He never put His foot inside a big city. He never traveled two hundred miles from the place He was born. He never did one of the things that usually accompany greatness. He had no credentials but Himself...

While still a young man, the tide of popular opinion turned against him. His friends ran away. One of them denied Him. He was turned over to His enemies. He went through the mockery of a trial. He was nailed upon a cross between two thieves. While He was dying His executioners gambled for the only piece of property He had on earth – His coat. When He was dead, He was laid in a borrowed grave through the pity of a friend.

Nineteen long centuries have come and gone, and today He is a centerpiece of the human race and leader of the column of progress.

I am far within the mark when I say that all the armies that ever marched, all the navies that were ever built; all the parliaments that ever sat and all the kings that ever reigned, put together, have not affected the life of man upon this earth as powerfully as has that one solitary life.

Another type of historical evidence for the validity of the Scriptures would be the application of common sense and logic to the testimony of Jesus Christ himself and his followers. Even unbelievers regard Jesus as a great moral teacher, probably the greatest of all time. But if Jesus were only a great moral teacher, and not really the Messiah and the Son of God He claimed to be, He would have been very deceitful or a lunatic, hardly the description of a man who forever changed the course of history and has been worshipped by billions of people since his death. In the words of C.S. Lewis (from his book, *Mere Christianity*), *"A man who was merely a man and said the sort of things Jesus said would not be a great moral teacher. He would either be a lunatic- on the level with the man who says he is a poached egg-or else he would be the Devil of Hell. You must make your choice. Either this man was, and is, the Son of God: or else a madman or something worse."*

Another reason I believe in the truth of the Christian Scriptures is that in actual practice Christianity works amazingly well for those who devote their lives to its teachings. Christian prayer has the power to dramatically transform and improve our lives, and many who convert to Christianity are rescued from the bondage of fear, unhappiness, and self-destructive lifestyles.

During my investigations over the past 10 years, I studied many extra-biblical sources of truth, including Near Death Experiences (NDE), world religions, paranormal experiences, quantum physics, mysticism, ancient and modern philosophy, and so on. After all that, I have concluded that the Christian Scriptures contain the absolute highest expression of human ideals, the noblest of which is unconditional, sacrificial love for all mankind, which is embodied in the God of the Bible and the life, teachings, and character of Jesus Christ.

Chapter 5

Extra-Biblical Truths about God

There seems to be a genuine paranoia among many Christian conservatives about investigating extra-Biblical sources of spiritual truth. These information sources include the discoveries of science, psychology, sociology, history, archaeology, metaphysics, and the scriptures of non-Christian religions. If the Bible contains accurate information about God, why on earth would you expect this to be contradicted by extra-Biblical sources of truth? Many churches sometimes attempt to control their flocks in a very "cultish" manner by exercising a form of "mind control." Church members are encouraged to submit to the spiritual "authority" of their leaders and avoid exposure to sources of truth outside of the Scriptures. They are especially warned to avoid those sources which seem to contradict their particular interpretation of the Scriptures.

In my view, they have got it just backwards. We shouldn't rely exclusively on the Scriptures to "authenticate" or "evaluate" the truths found outside of the Scriptures. Instead, we should be exploring those extra-Biblical sources of information in order to authenticate the truths found in the Bible. If you don't agree with this, ask yourself why you believe that the Bible is true in the first place. No religious text may be accepted as truth solely on the basis of its internal claims. In a court of law, the defendant is not declared innocent solely on the basis of his or her own testimony. That would be ludicrous. A proper defense can only be made by carefully examining many forms of evidence which are external to the statements of the defendant. This evidence would be historical and scientific in nature, but would also include the experiences and testimony of impartial observers.

At one point in my life, it was difficult for me to affirm the truths in Scripture while at the same time discarding the doctrine of inerrancy. This is no longer a problem for me for two reasons.

First, my investigation of extra-Biblical sources of information has provided strong evidence for the truths contained in the Scriptures.

Second, and equally important, this investigation has helped me to more correctly interpret and apply the truths of Scripture.

Truth is truth, no matter where you find it. All truth is God's truth. Many extra-Biblical truths are in my view reasonable, logical, and incontrovertible. Here are a few specific examples of how these extra-Biblical truths have influenced my theology and my interpretation of the Scriptures.

Extra-Biblical Truth Case Study No. 1:
The Stories in Genesis

When I was a young man, struggling with my faith, I desperately wanted to believe the Gospel of Christ and find assurance of my salvation. A huge obstacle for me was the difficulty I had accepting the literal truth of many Old Testament passages of Scripture, especially the creation account in Genesis and the events relating to human origins, the fall of man in the Garden of Eden, the flood story, the story of the Tower of Babel and the confusion of languages, and so on. I was completely unable to believe that they are literally true. As I read the narratives, they seemed rather absurd in many ways. Although I believed that God is completely able to circumvent and violate the laws of science, I couldn't believe that there would be any logical reason for Him to do so in the manner described in Genesis. Why would God choose to accomplish supernaturally what He could just as easily do through the natural processes which He had already set in motion? A bigger question for me was this. Why would God create the world is seven literal 24-hour days and then create a false geological, linguistic, cosmological, and archaeological history that would make it appear that the process occurred over billions of years? Why would God attempt to fool us in this way and in so doing make it nearly impossible for reputable scientists and rational thinkers to believe the Bible?

To make matters even worse, these stories lacked plausibility. Why would God need to rest on the seventh day? Why would God need to scoop up a handful of clay, or a rib from the side of Eve, to create the first male and female? Why would God, who is supposedly omniscient, be walking around in the garden calling out to Adam in order to find out where he was hiding? And a talking snake? Give me a break. If God wanted to destroy all mankind and start over, why would there be any need at all for the worldwide flood and the ark? Why not just snuff out all the bad guys instantaneously? This would eliminate the need to put millions of species of animals onto an ark that was not nearly big enough to accommodate them. Why would a man-made tower that reaches at most a few hundred feet into the air be such a threat to God? The confusion of languages at Babel seems not only unlikely but makes no sense at all. A confusion of languages would not at all be necessary in order to encourage mankind to spread out and explore their world. I could go on and on. These ancient stories bear all the earmarks of legend and myth, and they are contradicted by the findings of science, especially geology, cosmology, and paleontology.

If the stories in Genesis are not historically true and accurate, in what sense may they be relied upon for discovering truths about God and for guidance in making important life decisions? According to 2 Timothy 3:16, *"All Scripture is God-breathed and is useful for teaching, rebuking, correcting and training in righteousness..."* This passage says nothing about the Hebrew Bible (ie. the Old Testament) being historically accurate or literally true. In the Bible we find many different genres of literature, including historical narratives, legends, myths, poetry, songs, sermons and homilies, symbolism, imagery, parables, similes, and proverbs, none of which need to be scientifically or historically accurate in order to convey spiritual and moral truths. The Bible was derived from many oral and written sources, none of which originated with the intent of being incorporated into an infallible, inerrant book which would be identified by many as the authoritative word or words of God Himself. Their original intent and purpose was to communicate information that would motivate people to conduct their lives in a manner pleasing to God and beneficial to mankind.

So, with this in mind, what can we learn from extra-Biblical sources that will help us better understand, interpret and benefit from the stories and legends in the Book of Genesis? First of all, we learn from science, geology, linguistics, cosmology, and paleontology that the stories are not literally and historically true. Because of this, I personally would be reluctant to base any critical theological teaching on a literalistic interpretation of these stories. In order to believe Christian doctrines relating to observance of the Sabbath, capital punishment, the existence of Satan, original sin, human depravity, and so on, I personally would need to find support for those doctrines elsewhere in Scripture.

What we learn from archaeology is that these stories are a huge improvement over the creation myths and legends of the surrounding Babylonian and Sumerian cultures, from which they are partially derived. We see evidence of an evolution in thought. God is still described in largely anthropomorphic terms, but is now viewed as the creator of the universe, and He is a righteous God who enforces a moral code that will develop into something quite sophisticated over time.

Extra-Biblical Truth Case Study No. 2: God-Approved Genocide

Second only to the doctrine of eternal conscious torment (ECT) in Hell, God-approved genocide in the Bible has been the most troubling to me. If one believes in the inerrancy of the Bible, then one must also accept that genocide is an approved method of achieving God's purposes. Examples include the Genesis flood, the killing of all the first-born of Egypt prior to the Exodus, the subsequent conquest of Canaan, and God's continuing support of Israel in various wars against her enemies. The idea that God destroys His enemies in the form of mass genocide has, by extension, also found its way into the New Testament, especially in the Book of Revelation.

It's one matter to defend yourself against enemies who are seeking to kill you or your loved ones. It is quite another matter to employ the use of violence to advance a religious or territorial objective, especially when other options are equally available to you. Most Christian conservatives, who are strongly opposed to fundamentalist Islamic jihad on moral and ethical grounds, are perfectly comfortable with exactly the same methods being used by the nation of Israel in the Old Testament, and by God Himself in the Book of Revelation.

In the Bible, God is depicted as loving, yet at times very harsh in His judgments. God-approved Genocide has been rationalized as having a loving and redemptive purpose. The question then arises, does the end justify the means? When tempted to return evil for evil and employ violence to resolve problems or achieve righteous goals, are we able to do this in the spirit of what Christ taught us about loving our enemies and returning good for evil? Is there a conflict between what Christ taught and what was previously taught in the Old Testament? Was God really approving, even commanding, the use of genocide, or was man incorrectly ascribing this to God?

In order to successfully resolve this issue, we need to discard the doctrine of Scriptural inerrancy, and employ a different basis for the interpretation of Scripture. Separating truth from error in the Scriptures is not as difficult as you might expect. Those teachings which are consistent with what we know to be the true character of God, as described by Christ himself, may be accepted. Those teachings which are inconsistent with the true character of God must either be rejected or reinterpreted in ways that would resolve the discrepancies.

For the answer I seek, the primary extra-Biblical information source I would draw on is the use of common sense, logic, and the lessons of history. The answer that satisfies me most has to do with the concept of progressive revelation. I view the Bible as a man-made, yet God-inspired, record of an evolution of thought, a learning process. Through a process of trial and error we learn and grow in our personal lives. Even Jesus, Himself, started out with a blank slate and grew in wisdom and stature with both God and man. The same is true for humanity as a whole. Just as various plant and animal species develop and adapt through a process of God-directed macro and micro evolution, so it is with societies. God directs from behind the scenes. He works in and through us, not outside of us. Supernatural intervention is the exception, not the norm. He has chosen to accomplish His goals for mankind through us, not for us. He doesn't just hand us wisdom and all the answers to life in completed form, on a silver platter, as it were. Instead, He helps us to learn and grow in a better way, through actual human interactions. Spiritual, moral and ethical lessons are best learned first-hand, not second-hand, in the crucible of both positive and negative life experiences. In the Bible we find a record of this painful process on the societal level, and especially in the experience of one particular society which God has chosen to be an example for all the others, the nation of Israel. The Bible records their successes and their failures. It records their wisdom and also their misconceptions and misunderstandings.

This process reaches an apex of sorts in the life and teachings of Jesus Christ. All that has gone before should be evaluated on the basis of what Christ taught. Since the time of Christ, society has continued to evolve and change, and progress has not been easy or smooth. Many of Christ's followers have not been able to fully assimilate much of what He taught. Many of them remain stuck in the past and have not been able to discard many of the mistaken religious beliefs and ethical mores of the ancient Hebrews.

Extra-Biblical Truth Case Study No. 3: Soul Sleep

There are two main schools of thought regarding what happens to us immediately after death.

Some believe that the soul and body are so closely connected that when the body dies, so does the soul. When Christ comes again to earth, those who are dead in Christ (or "asleep," in the words of Paul) will be made alive again and their physical bodies will be resurrected and made immortal. Proponents of this view believe that non-Christians will also be resurrected, but at a much later date, at which time they will be either annihilated in the Lake of Fire or punished there for all eternity. Some, who subscribe to this view of the body-soul connection, believe that the Lake of Fire is symbolic of a purification and refinement process, after which all will eventually be saved and granted admission into the Kingdom of Heaven.

The second major school of thought is that the body and soul are separate and distinct, and the soul lives on in spiritual realms after the body dies. Some, who subscribe to this view, believe that punishments in Hell begin immediately after death. Some also believe that the purpose of those punishments is to bring sinners to repentance. Some believe that the "hellish" experiences after death are only temporary mental constructs and are not imposed by God.

A pretty good case from Scripture can be made for of the above views. I myself, subscribe to the latter view, and can make a strong case for it solely from Scripture. However, various extra-biblical sources of information also support my view.

According to virtually all NDE's (Near Death Experiences), the soul immediately leaves the body upon death and enters the spirit world (ie. heaven or heavens). If you believe that soul dies when the body dies, then you cannot at the same time believe that NDE's are valid out-of-body or after-death experiences. In my view, the evidence for the validity of NDE's is much stronger than the arguments against it. If you have not read up on this, I would encourage you read a few good books on the subject or research it on the internet. Most NDE experiencers testify that they were welcomed into the spirit world (ie. heaven) with open arms and experienced nothing but an overwhelming feeling of being loved unconditionally. This was true of both Christians and non-Christians, even atheists. Of the very small minority, who had "hellish" experiences, virtually all of them were eventually rescued as they called out for help.

Additional support for the immortality of the soul can be found in the findings of quantum physics. These findings support the view that the physical body is not actually physical at all, but is made up of particles which start out as waves and continually blink into and out of existence. Human consciousness is not an artifact of the physical body, but exactly the opposite. It exists independently from the quasi-physical body and actually creates all physical realities, solely through the power of observation. Some very excellent books have been written on this subject, in terms that the layman can understand. Many excellent YouTube videos have also been produced on the subject.

Extra-Biblical Truth Case Study No. 4:
Paul's Sermon on Mars Hill
and Progressive Revelation

Acts 17:22-31 *"So Paul stood in the midst of the Areopagus and said, 'Men of Athens, I observe that you are very religious in all respects. For while I was passing through and examining the objects of your worship, I also found an altar with this inscription, 'TO AN UNKNOWN GOD.' Therefore what you worship in ignorance, this I proclaim to you. The God who made the world and all things in it, since He is Lord of heaven and earth, does not dwell in temples made with hands; nor is He served by human hands, as though He needed anything, since He Himself gives to all people life and breath and all things; He made from one man every nation of mankind to live on all the face of the earth, having determined their appointed times and the boundaries of their habitation, they would seek God, if perhaps they might grope for Him and find Him, though He is not far from each one of us; in Him we live and move and exist, as even some of your own poets have said, 'For we also are His children.' Being then the children of God, we ought not to think that the Divine Nature is like gold or silver or stone, an image formed by the art and thought of man. Therefore having overlooked the times of ignorance, God is now declaring to men that all people everywhere should repent, because He has fixed a day in which He will judge the world in righteousness through a Man whom He has appointed, having furnished proof to all men by raising Him from the dead.'"*

From this passage it appears that Paul believed that all mankind originated with one man, although the word "man" is not in the original Greek. He was presumably speaking about Adam. Paul was a product of his age and was probably a Biblical literalist. At the time he preached the above sermon in Athens, he also probably believed in a future judgment of all mankind on a single, fixed day in the future. I believe all human beings on Earth are descended from a single man and woman, but I don't believe this because of the Genesis myth. Instead, I believe it because it has been discovered scientifically through mitochondrial DNA analysis. It has also been established by science that other human beings existed prior to the "mitochondrial Eve," from whom all present day humans are descended. It has been estimated that our current lineage branched off from the rest of humanity between 100,000 and 200,000 years ago. So, it appears that Paul didn't know everything there was to know about human origins.

Paul's sermon also raises another difficulty. His teaching that God will judge all mankind in a single *"appointed day"* in the future is contradicted by the NDE (Near Death Experience) during which, at least for many of us, a "life review" or "self-judgment" occurs almost immediately after death, and it appears that we for the most

41

part judge ourselves and are not judged by God at all. This reminds me of the saying in John 3:17 that *"God did not send his Son into the world to condemn the world, but to save the world through him."* Paul also seems to contradict his teaching of a universal judgment in the future when He says in 1 Cor. 5:8 that *"to be absent from the body is to be at home with the Lord."* Early on in his ministry, I'm sure that Paul believed in the imminent return of Jesus to Earth to judge all mankind and set up an earthly kingdom. As time went by, this hope faded and was replaced by another concept, that of a spiritual kingdom, not of this Earth. The seeds of this belief may also be found in the Paul's above sermon on Mars Hill, where he states that God is not a physical being who dwells in physical places. Instead, God exists everywhere including inside all of us. *"In Him we live and move and exist"* and *"we also are all His children."* This obviously refers to non-Christians, as well as Christians, as Paul was speaking to non-Christian Athenians.

Eventually, the focus of the early Christian community shifted from an emphasis on a physical Kingdom to that of a spiritual Kingdom which exists everywhere. This transition did not occur at the same time for all the writers of the New Testament. The idea that Jesus' kingdom is *"not of this world"* was introduced later on, and may only be found in the Gospel of John, the last of the Gospels to be written (See John 18:36). Even Jesus, Himself, in my view, probably did not come to this realization until late in His ministry, perhaps not until after His resurrection. According to Paul's sermon above, God's revelations to mankind are progressive in nature. In the past, mankind has been kept pretty much in the dark about many spiritual matters and it was determined by God that *"they would seek God, if perhaps they might grope for Him and find Him, though He is not far from each one of us."* Because of this, God *"overlooks our ignorance."* God apparently judges us only on the basis of what He has revealed to us.

In the following passage in 2 Corinthians, Paul suggests that the *"judgment seat of Christ"* occurs for each of us immediately upon death, rather than as a single mass judgment day in the distant future.

2 Cor. 5:1-10 "For we know that if the earthly tent we live in is destroyed, we have a building from God, an eternal house in heaven, not built by human hands. [2] Meanwhile we groan, longing to be clothed instead with our heavenly dwelling, [3] because when we are clothed, we will not be found naked. [4] For while we are in this tent, we groan and are burdened, because we do not wish to be unclothed but to be clothed instead with our heavenly dwelling, so that what is mortal may be swallowed up by life. [5] Now the one who has fashioned us for this very purpose is God, who has given us the Spirit as a deposit, guaranteeing what is to come. [6] Therefore we are always confident and know that as long as we are at home in the body we are away from the Lord. [7] For we live by faith, not by sight. [8] We are confident, I say, and would prefer to be away from the body and at home with the Lord. [9] So we make it our goal to please him, whether we are at home in the body or away from it. [10] For we must all appear before the judgment seat of Christ, so that each of us may receive what is due us for the things done while in the body, whether good or bad."

So, what do we learn from all of this?

My first take-a-way is that the progressive nature of God's revelation to us did not stop with the life of Christ, but continued afterwards. I believe this process continues today, and I would expect that with further advances in science, parapsychology and various forms of critical analysis of the Scriptures themselves we can gain additional insights that will help us better understand the true nature of God and the purpose for our existence here on Earth.

My second take-a-way is that the Christian Scriptures, though not inerrant, are still useful for *"teaching, rebuking, correcting and training in righteousness."* They do not provide us with definitive and incontrovertible answers to the exact nature of the afterlife and what happens after death. A great deal of mystery still remains. According to Paul's sermon above, up until the time of Christ, God was OK with our not having all the answers. Our understanding has grown since then, but we still have a long ways to go. I'm sure God is OK with that. Is there value in not knowing all the answers, or having to dig for them, at the very least? I would assume so.

Extra-Biblical Truth Case Study No. 5: The Holy Spirit

You might never have thought of it this way, but the Holy Spirit of God is actually an extra-Biblical source of information. According to John 16:13, the Holy Spirit "will guide you into all truth." In John 14:26, Jesus said, *"the Advocate, the Holy Spirit, whom the Father will send in my name, will teach you all things and will remind you of everything I have said to you."*

The question I have for you is this. If the Scriptures are self-explanatory and easy to interpret, why do we need the Holy Spirit? The truth is that the Scriptures are in many places self-contradictory and contain a mixture of truth and error. I'm not at all sure that Christ ever intended His teachings to be written down by fallible men and then passed on to others as the actual words of God Himself. If we are going to make sense of the Scriptures and benefit from them, we need to seek guidance from the original source on which the Scriptures themselves are based. The Scriptures are first, second and third-hand accounts of the working of the Holy Spirit in the lives of fallible men. I realize that this sounds like a rather negative and cynical view of Scripture. But we must remember that we don't worship a book. We worship a living God who is more than able to directly interact with us truthfully and intimately. He will not lead us astray if we seek Him with an open heart and good intentions.

Rather than trusting in the guidance of the Holy Spirit when interpreting Scripture, most Christians have ceded this God-given right to their religious authorities. Instead of trusting in their own intellect and intuition under the guidance of the Holy Spirit, they have decided to let their pastors and teachers do all their thinking for them. The problem is that most of those pastors and teachers have done the same thing. So we basically have the blind leading the blind, resulting in many contradictory Christian belief systems and denominations, with many factions accusing others of blasphemy and heresy.

So, the question is this. Would the situation be better if every individual Christian decided to take back their God-given right to access spiritual knowledge directly from the original source, the Holy Spirit? At first glance, one might conclude that this would result in even more disunity and an even greater variety of competing beliefs. I believe exactly the opposite would happen, and here's why.

Let me begin by using a secular example. Totalitarian ideologies are only able to deceive their subjects in the absence the free flow of information. They implement massive propaganda campaigns, and don't allow their subjects access to a free press, or travel outside their borders. The idea is that the masses are too ignorant to make good decisions. They aren't capable of thinking for themselves. They will all be better off if they allow their leaders to do their thinking for them. Due in no small part to the free flow of information across national borders, totalitarianism has gradually been giving way to democracy in many parts of the world. The most successful nations in the world today are the democracies. They are imperfect, but not nearly as bad as the totalitarian systems.

The same is true with respect to the Christian religion. Various denominational leaders strive to maintain a rigid orthodoxy in their respective groupings. They do this primarily by restricting the free flow of information and threatening dissidents within their ranks with excommunication and damnation in Hell. As long as these leaders are successful in maintaining their ecclesiastical authority and their status as gatekeepers of spiritual truth, the Christian church will remain divided and will become increasingly isolated from the popular culture. They will continue to lose ground to advances in spiritual growth and evolution that are currently taking place in the popular culture.

Here's what I believe. As more and more people begin to question their religious authorities and seek to guidance of the Holy Spirit instead, two things will begin to happen.

First, it will become apparent that no one knows all the truth. People will have to humbly admit that there is more that they don't know than what they do know. They will be less dogmatic in their thinking and far less judgmental of those who disagree with them.

Secondly, common threads of truth will begin to emerge as people begin to realize that the most important truths are those which the Holy Spirit reveals to all of them, truths relating to the loving, forgiving and just nature of God and the importance of developing and expressing in our lives qualities of character like love, kindness, justice, mercy and forgiveness.

Christian scholars and leaders will still play an important role, but they will exercise their roles with more tolerance and humility. The Christian church will become more inclusive and far more effective in leading back to Christ those who have lost their way.

Chapter 6

Christian Salvation

Is the experience of Christian salvation instantaneous or a process?

Between 1900 and 1925, Russell Conwell delivered his famous speech, *"Acres of Diamonds,"* over 5,000 times. In this speech Russell told stories of people who sold their lands and went off in search of riches, only to find out later that great riches were discovered on the lands that they had left. The most prominent story in this lecture is about a Persian by the name of Ali Hafed, who sold his farm and used up all the money from the sale during a world-wide search for diamonds. Eventually he spent all his money, ended up destitute and committed suicide. Afterwards, diamonds were discovered on the property that he had sold, and that farm became the site of the largest diamond mine in the world. That reminds me somewhat of a story that Jesus told of a Prodigal Son who took his inheritance ahead of schedule and left home. After squandering his inheritance he became destitute. Unlike the stories in Russell Conwell's speech, however, this story had a happy ending. The Prodigal Son eventually found true riches, but not until after returning home.

The Kingdom of God is not something a person finds away from home. It may only be found within. I believe with all my heart that all were saved on the Cross of Calvary, because Jesus died for the sins of all humanity. *"He Himself is the propitiation for our sins; and not for ours only, but also for those of the whole world"* (1 John 2:2). *"God is the Savior of all men, and especially of those who believe"* (1 Timothy 4:10). According to 1 Cor. 15:22, *"all will be made alive in Christ."* Not only were we all saved on the Cross of Calvary, but we were at the same time raised up with

47

Christ and seated with Him in the heavenly realms. *"God raised us up with Christ and seated us with him in the heavenly realms in Christ Jesus"* (Ephesians 2:6).

The point I am making here is that Salvation in Christ is something everyone already possesses. The problem is most people are unaware of it and are not able to experience it. The experience of Christian salvation is described in the Bible as a past, present and future event, depending on which aspect of the salvation experience is being referred to. After all, Christ saves us from many different things, and we are saved from these things at different times. Some of the things Christ saves us from have not even occurred yet. In the mind of God, who is able to view the past, present and future as a single event, salvation may be viewed as occurring instantaneously. But from our human perspective, we view and experience our salvation as various stages of a process which plays out over time. In the broadest sense the term "salvation" refers to many different experiences and events, culminating in the final event at the end of the ages when all are completely redeemed and glorified in Heaven.

To some, salvation means to have eternal life, which they would define as "unending conscious existence." As I point out elsewhere in this book, that definition of salvation is based on an incorrect translation of the Greek word *"aionian,"* which actually means the opposite of eternal and everlasting. It refers to a limited period of time, or an age, with a beginning and an end. This definition of salvation is also erroneous because the word *"zoe,"* or "life," does not in this context refer to physical or conscious life. Those who receive *"aionian"* life during their earthly existence are already conscious and alive physically. *"Aionian"* life to refers to spiritual life, not physical or conscious life. Although *"aionian"* life may be experienced in the present, it may only be experienced partially. Spiritual life, or fellowship with God, is something that we grow into. For some, this spiritual awakening begins suddenly during dramatic conversion experience. Others grow into relationship with Christ more gradually and are not able to identify a specific point in time when they were converted. Right now we see Christ only

48

through the eyes of faith, as in a mirror darkly, but some day we will meet Him face to face and will know Him fully (1 Cor. 13:12). Most Christians would agree that an important component of Christian salvation is being made spiritually alive in Christ during one's earthly existence. The mistake most of us make is adding an everlasting time component to it. All Christians will indeed live forever, and so won't everyone else. Conscious existence does not end with the death of the physical body.

Another very important component of Christian Salvation has to do with the forgiveness of sin and being saved from the power that sin has over us. No one can be completely saved in this lifetime with respect to gaining victory over the sin in their lives. Believers are admonished in 1 John 1:9 to confess their sins and seek God's cleansing on a regular basis. We still struggle with sin in our lives (see Romans 6-8). *"If we say we have no sin, we deceive ourselves and the truth is not in us."* (1 John 1:8) While it is true that Jesus died for our sins on Calvary, we still suffer the temporal consequences of our sin and still experience the righteous judgments of God in this life and the next. The purpose of our Heavenly Father's chastisement is to refine and purify us and mold us into the image of Christ. This aspect of Christian salvation does not happen instantaneously.

The final component of Christian salvation is the experience of the ultimate redemption and glorification of our souls in Heaven. Obviously, none of us are currently saved in this sense. In the following Scripture passage, the Apostle Paul describes this aspect of our salvation as something we experience only partially in this life.

"I consider that our present sufferings are not worth comparing with the glory that will be revealed in us. For the creation waits in eager expectation for the children of God to be revealed. For the creation was subjected to frustration, not by its own choice, but by the will of the one who subjected it, in hope that the creation itself will be liberated from its bondage to decay and brought into the freedom and glory of the children of God. We know that the whole

49

creation has been groaning as in the pains of childbirth right up to the present time. Not only so, but we ourselves, who have the firstfruits of the Spirit, groan inwardly as we wait eagerly for our adoption to sonship, the redemption of our bodies. For in this hope we were saved. But hope that is seen is no hope at all. Who hopes for what they already have? But if we hope for what we do not yet have, we wait for it patiently. (Romans 8:18-25)

Does the salvation process continue into the next life?

Romans 8:29: *"For those whom He foreknew, He also predestined to become conformed to the image of His Son."*

God's ultimate goal is to transform each of us into the image of Christ. I believe this refers not only to giving us spiritual bodies like Christ, but the shaping of our characters as well. This being the case, I would assume that God will not be finished with us immediately after we die, when we receive our spiritual bodies.

Paul referred to some of the Christians in Corinth as *mere "babes in Christ"* (1 Cor. 3:1), and some of them were sick and dying because of their sin (1 Cor. 11:30). It is obvious from these passages, and from simple observation, that Christians do not enter life after death with fully reformed characters. Some, perhaps most, Christians think that our basic character will be instantly changed at the rapture, when our bodies are transformed, but is this really the case? If God were to change our characters instantly in this way, the only way He could do it would be to reprogram our brains, as with a computer or robot. Would the result be an authentic change in character, or the loss of genuine character, instead? Only through real and genuine life experiences can we develop genuine qualities of character, especially that of *Agape* love which involves by definition sacrifice and selfless acts of kindness. Also, an important facet of genuine love is empathy, or the ability to feel what others are feeling and identify with the sufferings of others. This can only be genuinely learned from actual human experience.

50

If God were to instantly create these attitudes, feelings and qualities of character, without exposing us to the actual living conditions under which they are authentically produced, they would not be real, in my view. That is why, when he created us, he placed us in a flawed world and gave us the freedom to make both right and wrong choices, suffer the consequences of those decisions, and in the process develop genuine qualities of character. One of my favorite Scripture passages that describes this process is found in the book of James:

James 1:2-3 *"Consider it pure joy, my brothers whenever you face trials of many kinds, because you know that the testing of your faith develops perseverance. Perseverance must finish its work so that you may be mature and complete, not lacking anything."*

According to the above passage, *"perseverance must finish its work."* If this work has not been finished by the time you die, then it may logically be assumed that more time will be required after death. If we view salvation as a process, rather than an instantaneous event, then the warning that James gives in Chapter two of his epistle regarding the relationship between faith and works would apply to Christians, even after death. We are saved by faith, not of works, but our salvation is an ages-long process and will not be complete until our character fully conforms to that of Christ.

Sometimes the Bible expresses truths from a positional point of view, from the viewpoint of our position in Christ. Positionally, according to Ephesians 2:6, we have already been seated with Christ in the heavenly places. From God's point of view, who can view the events of history from a timeless perspective, the process of our transformation into the likeness of Christ has already been accomplished. He views us *"in Christ"* through the cross of Calvary. But in our human experience, we view this transformation as a process that occurs over time. Especially in the writings of Paul, many of these truths about our relationship with Christ are expressed as positional truth, while at other times they are

51

expressed as experiential truth. These conflicting views of our salvation may be easily resolved if you view salvation as a continuing process from our human experiential perspective, but a completed process from God's perspective.

Positional vs. Experiential Truth

Romans 8:18-25:

"I consider that our present sufferings are not worth comparing with the glory that will be revealed in us. For the creation waits in eager expectation for the children of God to be revealed. For the creation was subjected to frustration, not by its own choice, but by the will of the one who subjected it, in hope that the creation itself will be liberated from its bondage to decay and brought into the freedom and glory of the children of God.

We know that the whole creation has been groaning as in the pains of childbirth right up to the present time. Not only so, but we ourselves, who have the firstfruits of the Spirit, groan inwardly as we wait eagerly for our adoption to sonship, the redemption of our bodies. For in this hope we were saved. But hope that is seen is no hope at all. Who hopes for what they already have? But if we hope for what we do not yet have, we wait for it patiently."

In the past, I felt that the above passage of Scripture should not be taken literally. I presumed that *"all creation"* would include both animate and inanimate objects. How can an inanimate object *"wait with eager expectation"* or *"groan?"* After much study and contemplation, not only of the Scriptures, but also of physics, I have come to realize that the above passage of Scripture may be accepted as literal truth. Consider the following passages of Scripture which deal with both the omni-presence and creative activity of God, in the person of Jesus Christ. In the Bible, God the Father and Jesus the Christ are used interchangeably, two distinct personalities but one in essence. The third person on the Trinity,

52

the Holy Spirit, is also used to describe both God the Father and Jesus Christ interchangeably.

"You, however, are not in the realm of the flesh but are in the realm of the Spirit, if indeed the Spirit of God lives in you. And if anyone does not have the Spirit of Christ, they do not belong to Christ." Romans 8:9

"For in him (Christ) *all things were created: things in heaven and on earth, visible and invisible, whether thrones or powers or rulers or authorities; all things have been created through him and for him."* Colossians 1:16

"'For in him (God the Father) we live and move and have our being.' As some of your own poets have said, 'We are his offspring.' Acts 17:28

God's creation is "separate" from God Himself only in the sense that Jesus Christ is Separate from God the Father. Jesus is God's offspring, His only begotten Son. Well, guess what? We are also God's offspring, according to Acts 17:28 (see above). We are actually divine, in the same sense that Jesus Christ is divine, except that we are "begotten" of Christ and are made up of "Christ parts," Because Christ is in turn made up of "God parts," we would by extension also have divine natures. We do have separate and distinct personalities, but we are made of the same "stuff" (spirit) as the triune Godhead. I also believe that all creation, including both animate and inanimate objects and entities, are part of God. Another way of terming this would be to say that we are all "manifestations" of God. Nothing is separate from God Himself. God is omnipresent. There is nowhere that God is not. We are all intimately connected with God, and with each other for that matter.

So why does the Bible describe humanity as "lost," or "separated from God," or "under condemnation," or "enemies of God?" The reason is that most of us are not consciously aware of our divine natures. We are not aware of God's presence in our lives. We have no conscious relationship with God. We live in the "Hells" of our own making. We are separated from God only in our conscious awareness, or should I say, lack thereof. There is no place we can go, or be sent, where we can escape the presence of God.

I like to distinguish between our "true spiritual selves" and our "fleshly self-unawarenes" (See Romans 7) by using the terms "positional" and "experiential" truth. Positionally, we have divine, spiritual natures, and were redeemed by the blood of Christ on Calvary, and have been raised up with Christ and reside with Him in the heavenly realms. (See Eph. 2:6). Most non-Christians are not at all aware of this. Christians have experienced these positional truths only partially, and have experienced only the "first fruits" of the Spirit.

POSITIONAL:	EXPERIENTIAL:
Alive	Dead
Spiritual	Fleshly/Carnal
Redeemed	Under condemnation
At home	Lost
Cleansed from sin	In need of forgiveness
Saved	Unsaved
Children of God	Children of Satan
United with God/Christ	Separated from God/Christ

Both Christians and non-Christians are in a process of transition from one mental state to the other. The process of Christian salvation is not instantaneous. It is an ages-long growth process. No one is completely "saved" or "lost." The Spirit of God is at work in our lives before, during, and after our profession of faith in

54

Christ. All are at some stage in a process which culminates at the end of the ages. In the end, everyone will be presented faultless before the throne of God, and every knee will bow to Christ and acknowledge Him as Lord, and God will become *"all in all"* in everyone's conscious awareness. (See 1 Cor. 15:22-28)

Chapter 7

The Atonement

Regarding our "Sin Debt"

My father once told me that whatever He gave to me I owe to my children, not to him. We don't owe God anything. Instead, we owe it all to the rest of God's children. I have been forgiven much, and I need to pass that forward. The purpose of God's so-called punishments is to correct us and lead us to repentance. God has always been, and always will be, our loving heavenly Father. Calvary did not change the way God deals with us and our sinfulness. It changed the way we view God, as a loving Father who gives to us sacrificially without wanting anything more from us than our love and gratitude. He wants this for our benefit, not His. What He wants for us is that we learn to love others as He loves us. When we learn to do this our lives will be wonderfully transformed as we identify with the Christ of Calvary and begin to think and act like Him.

The Purpose of Animal Sacrifices

The system of making animal sacrifices to appease an angry God was inherited by the Hebrews from previous and surrounding cultures. It is not the blood of animal sacrifices that cleanses us from sin. Instead, it is the attitude of repentance that accompanies those sacrifices.

See Isaiah 1:11: *"The multitude of your sacrifices-- what are they to me?" says the LORD. "I have more than enough of burnt offerings, of rams and the fat of fattened animals; I have no pleasure in the blood of bulls and lambs and goats."*

Also see Hosea 6:6: *"For I desire mercy, not sacrifice, and acknowledgment of God rather than burnt offerings."*

The Old Testament sacrifices were a type or symbol of what was to come in the person of Jesus Christ. The "blood" of Christ, I believe, is also a symbol of a deeper truth, that Godly love is sacrificial in nature. *"Agape"* love is by definition sacrificial. It costs you something. In the case of Calvary, the cost was Jesus' life.

So, when the writer of Hebrews says that *"without the shedding of blood there is no remission of sin,"* (Heb. 9:22) he is referring not to the physical act of killing an animal, but to the change of heart that accompanies it. The same is true for Christ's sacrifice on Calvary. It was not the physical shedding of Christ's blood that made atonement for our sins. Instead it was the underling truths that the blood atonement represented. God in the person of His Son, Jesus, identified Himself with our sin and shame and took upon Himself the burden of our sin. When we look to the cross for mercy and forgiveness, we are forgiven and freed from the bondage that sin holds over us.

The Atonement

The cross of Calvary is God's way of identifying with us through an incredible act of humility and submission. This was God's way of demonstrating His love for us. *"But God demonstrates his own love for us in this: While we were still sinners, Christ died for us."* (Rom. 5:8) You don't really understand a person, and cannot fully appreciate that person's pain and suffering, unless you have actually walked in his/her shoes. The real message of Calvary is exactly the opposite of what most evangelicals preach. Instead of a super Holy and separate God requiring the blood of men to appease His anger and satisfy the demands of justice, we instead see God Himself in the person of His Son, Jesus, humbling Himself and literally becoming one with us in our suffering and pain. Not only is God able to look upon sin and abide in the presence of sin, He actually became sin for our benefit, in the person of Jesus Christ. *"God made him who had no sin to be sin for us, so that in him we might become the righteousness of God."* (2 Cor. 5:21)

On Calvary, God has demonstrated to us that literally nothing can separate us from His love. No matter how sinful and unworthy we might think we are, none of us is so bad that God cannot love us and actually live in us. The feelings that we have of isolation from God and abandonment by God are illusions. Christian Salvation may best be regarded as getting rid of the illusion and experiencing God's presence in our lives. We are not saved from the wrath of God, but from our failure to understand how loving and understanding God really is. Our God is indeed a God of wrath, but the object of His wrath is godlessness and wickedness, because these things are harmful to us, the objects of His love. *"The wrath of God is being revealed from heaven against all the godlessness and wickedness of people, who suppress the truth by their wickedness."* (Romans 1:18) God hates sin, not sinners. Rather than separating Himself from us because of our sin, He is present with us through all our sinning, trials and suffering.

The penalty for sin is spiritual death, or estrangement from God. This is not a permanent condition. That which is dead can be made alive again. Christians, who were once dead in their sins, have been made alive in Christ. According to Ephesians 2:4-5, *"because of his great love for us, God, who is rich in mercy, made us alive with Christ even when we were dead in transgressions—it is by grace you have been saved."* See also Romans 6:1-11. If the penalty for sin were everlasting torture in a place called Hell, then Jesus could not possibly have paid the price of our sins on Calvary. He rose from the dead less than three days later and is very much alive today in Heaven, not Hell.

Jesus' purpose in coming to Earth was to redeem all mankind from sin and death. *"For God did not send his Son into the world to condemn the world, but to save the world through him."* (John 3:17) On Calvary, Jesus acted as a surrogate for all mankind, when He endured estrangement from God and died both spiritually and physically. According to 1 John 2:2, *"He himself is the propitiation for our sins; and not for ours only, but also for those of the whole world."*

The difference between those of us who are saved and those who are not saved has to do with our awareness and experience of the connection that we all have with God through Christ. God is omnipresent and exists everywhere, including in the hearts of all mankind. When we by faith enter into relationship with the Christ of Calvary, we are awakened to this connection and experience God's love, mercy and forgiveness in a personal way.

The Participatory Atonement
vs. the Substitutionary Atonement

The "suffering servant" of Isaiah 53 originally referred only to the nation of Israel, not the Messiah. To this day, that is the interpretation accepted by most Jews. The nation of Israel was being punished for their iniquities and at the same time they were being healed by it. The purpose of God's judgments on the nation of Israel was not retribution but refinement and purification, and in the end they are healed and restored.

Christians saw in this passage a foreshadowing of the cross of Christ. By substituting Christ for the Nation of Israel, they came up with the idea of a "substitutionary atonement," whereby Christ takes the place of the nation of Israel and suffers in their stead. There is no doubt that most early Christians saw it this way, as most of them do to this day. On the surface, this seems to be what happened at Calvary.

The Apostle Paul, I believe, saw a deeper meaning. We are not cleansed by what Christ did on Calvary on our behalf, but instead by our PARTICIPATION in His death and resurrection. All of us, like the Hebrew nation, suffer for our iniquities, the purpose of which is to refine and purify us. The difference with Jesus is that he did not suffer for his own iniquities, but ours. He identified Himself with our sin, took upon Himself our humanity, and suffered the consequences of our sin right along with us. The atonement that took place on Calvary does not mean that we do not suffer for our iniquities. It means that Christ suffers with us, forgives us, and lifts us up to new life TOGETHER WITH HIM in Heaven. If God had chastised Christ "instead of" or "on behalf of" us, then He would not still be chastising Christians today. God chastises those whom He loves, and He loves all of us, Christians and non-Christians alike.

In Romans 6:1-14, the Apostle Paul elaborates on this:

"What shall we say, then? Shall we go on sinning so that grace may increase? By no means! We are those who have died to sin; how can we live in it any longer? Or don't you know that all of us who were baptized into Christ Jesus were baptized into his death? We were therefore buried with him through baptism into death in order that, just as Christ was raised from the dead through the glory of the Father, we too may live a new life.

For if we have been united with him in a death like his, we will certainly also be united with him in a resurrection like his. For we know that our old self was crucified with him so that the body ruled by sin might be done away with, that we should no longer be slaves to sin— because anyone who has died has been set free from sin.

Now if we died with Christ, we believe that we will also live with him. For we know that since Christ was raised from the dead, he cannot die again; death no longer has mastery over him. The death he died, he died to sin once for all; but the life he lives, he lives to God.

In the same way, count yourselves dead to sin but alive to God in Christ Jesus. Therefore do not let sin reign in your mortal body so that you obey its evil desires. Do not offer any part of yourself to sin as an instrument of wickedness, but rather offer yourselves to

God as those who have been brought from death to life; and offer every part of yourself to him as an instrument of righteousness. For sin shall no longer be your master, because you are not under the law, but under grace.

Theories of the Atonement

Exactly what it was that Christ accomplished on Calvary has been a matter of fierce debate among Christian scholars over the centuries. My view is this. What was accomplished was the salvation of all mankind. By what mechanism was this accomplished? That is what the debate is all about. There are several predominant theories of the atonement. I would briefly summarize them as follows, in laymen's language:

1. Christ's death was a ransom paid by God to Himself or the Devil in exchange for mankind's redemption,

2. Christ's death was substituted for ours, thereby cancelling our sin debt and making it possible for God to forgive us without our having to be righteous on our own accord,

3. Christ's death was a demonstration of God's sacrificial love, by which God exerts moral influence to woo us into relationship with Himself,

4. Christ's death and resurrection was a demonstration to mankind that there is life after death, that God has always loved and accepted us. God was revealing that to us on Calvary what has always been the case.

5. Christ's death and resurrection is a process that we all go through. Because we are all spiritually united with Christ, we actually experienced it simultaneously with Christ. This is what I have termed the "participatory" view of the atonement. The term "participatory" is one that I have coined.

There are elements of truth in all of the above theories.

The participatory view, I believe, is that which most closely aligns with the writings of the Apostle Paul and the teachings of Jesus. That is why Paul talks so much about being "in Christ" and Christ being "in us." That is what Paul is talking about when he talks about our identification with, and participation with Christ in His death, burial and resurrection. Jesus made the point several times that a seed must die before it can grow and reproduce, that death precedes life. In order to be born again (of the spirit), the body must die. Paul said that this can be experienced before we die, as well, when we repent of our sin and die to our old nature and identify with Christ in His death and resurrection. So it is about this life as well as the next.

When Paul says that Christ died "for" us, he wasn't saying the Christ died "in our place" or "instead of us." He was saying that Christ died "for our benefit." How do we benefit from Christ's death and resurrection? Well, He took us along with Himself and raised us up together with Himself. He carried us on His own back, so to speak. He said that when He would be lifted up, He would draw (literally "drag") ALL men to Himself. When Paul says the righteousness of Christ is "imputed" to us, he wasn't saying that we exchanged our righteousness for that of Christ. He was saying that the righteousness of Christ was "transferred" to us as we participated with Him in His death, burial and resurrection. It was given to us by grace, through no merit of our own. The ransom that Christ paid was not to God or the Devil. It was simply the price He had to pay in order to put Himself in the position of dying and rising up again with us and for us.

This does not mean that we don't experience death, nor does it mean that we don't experience the loving chastisements of God for our sins. What it means is that Christ is the one who carries us through the process. Our salvation results from Christ's initiative, and the good that we do we cannot take credit for, because it is all done under the influence and in the power of Christ's Spirit. In order for Christ to do this work, it was necessary that He die with us. Not only did He die with us, He also was raised from the grave and exalted in the Heavenly places with us.

Christian salvation is something that happened in Christ. What we refer to as "getting saved" is temporal process in this life whereby we "experience" in our conscious awareness something that has already happened to us in Christ.

The other side of the coin of "participatory atonement" is this. Not only did we participate in the death and resurrection of Christ, but He also currently participates in our death and resurrection during our sojourn on here on earth. The term "Christ in us" refers to the idea that God the Father, as the Christ, lives in us. He not only lives in us. He is us. We all share the divine nature. We are all sparks of the divine, God's children, as it were. We are all connected. We are separated from God and one another only in the sense that we are unaware of our connectedness. Yes, we all have separate and distinct personalities or egos, but at the same time we are all part of a single divine godhead.

As an aside, I would like to point out that the term "Christ in us" does not refer uniquely to Christians. It refers the fact that Christians are aware of this connection and have invited the Spirit of Christ to take control. All are indwelt by Christ and all share the divine nature, but not all are aware of it. For all practical purposes, Christ might as well not be there if we are not aware of His presence and if we fail to exploit the power of the His Spirit within us to overcome the weakness of the flesh and live up to our calling.

The Apostle Paul did say, in Romans 8:9, that *"you, however, are not in the realm of the flesh but are in the realm of the Spirit, if indeed the Spirit of God lives in you. And if anyone does not have the Spirit of Christ, they do not belong to Christ."* This does not mean that only Christians are indwelt by Christ. Both God the Father and the Christ are omnipresent. There is nowhere that God does not dwell. What Paul is saying is that God is not there in the practical sense if we do not allow Him to take control of our lives. He lives in us in the active sense only to the extent that we allow

Him to live His life through us. Christ does not belong to us unless we take possession of Him and lay claim to Him. God always was, still is, and always will be our loving Heavenly Father. But in the practical sense, He might as well not be if we are not aware of it and go our own way into the foreign country, as in the case of the Prodigal Son. When we are ready to return home and reclaim our birthright, our Heavenly Father will still be there waiting for us.

Chapter 8

The Trinity

A very strong case can be made from Scripture for both the Unitarian and the Trinitarian views. I won't bore you with the details. You can easily learn about the arguments on both sides from other sources. What I will attempt to do is reconcile the two based on simple logic. Many of my comments in this essay are speculative in nature. At the same time, I have tried to remain true to the Scriptures.

Let's begin with the assumption that the writers of the Bible were inspired and have communicated to us the basic truths of the matter. Most of the Scriptures in support of each view appear to be quite unambiguous and for the most part clearly stated. So I would have to assume that both the Unitarian and Trinitarian views are true and compatible with one another, hence we are dealing with a paradox, not necessarily a contradiction.

It is clear from many statements of Christ himself that He and the Father are not one and the same, and that God the Father is greater than the Son (John 14:28). Jesus prayed to the Father (Mark 1:35). He gave God the Father credit for the performance of His miracles (John 14:10). He was not omniscient (Matthew 24:36), and He had to learn about God much in the same way that we do (Luke 2:52). He had to grow in wisdom and favor with both God and Man. He was definitely separated from the Father and wouldn't return to the Father until after His death, burial and resurrection (John 20:17). He even said He was not good and that only the Father in Heaven is good (Luke 18:19). He prayed in Gethsemane for God to remove the *"cup"* of suffering that He was facing, and God turned Him down (Luke 22:42). He referred to Himself as the Son of Man, not the Son of God (Matthew 18:11), and never once directly and unambiguously claimed to be God Himself. He made statements about the oneness He experienced with the Father, but then went on to explain how all of us could experience the same (John 17:21).

On the other hand, He was given the name *"Emmanuel,"* which means *"God with us"* (Matt. 1:23). He did describe Himself with the term *"I AM,"* a designation which refers to God Himself, and that He pre-existed Abraham (Jn. 8:58). He is referred to by the writers of the New Testament as the only begotten Son of God (Jn. 3:16), and as the Alpha and Omega, the beginning and the end (Rev. 22:13), which implies that He existed at the beginning of time and also at the end of time. In other words, He, like God the Father, is co-eternal. He did say, *"I and the Father are one"* (Jn10:27). He allowed Himself to be worshipped by His followers after His resurrection. When Thomas called Him *"my Lord and My God,"* Jesus did not reprimand him (Jn. 20:28). He was worshipped by His followers (Matt. 14:33; 28:9) and at the end of the ages every knee will bow to Him and worship Him (Phil. 2:9-11). His *"equality"* with the Father prior to His incarnation is described in Phil. 2:6.

So how could both of the above descriptions of Christ be true? We won't find a detailed discussion of this issue in the Bible. As a matter of fact, the deity of Christ did not become codified and clearly spelled out in the form of official creeds until centuries after the Bible was written. So, let's get one thing straight from the beginning. Your eternal destiny doesn't depend on which view you take regarding this controversy. If it were that important, I'm sure that the writers of the Bible would have spelled it out much more clearly and talked about it a whole lot more than they did. What they did believe was that Jesus was unique and one of a kind, the *"only begotten"* Son of God (Jn. 3:16), and that He made atonement for the sins of the world on the cross of Calvary (1 Jn. 2:2). He is *the "way, the truth, and the life,"* and all roads to the Father go through Him (Jn. 14:6). There is no other way to the Father except through Jesus Christ. He is the *"door"* through whom we must pass in order to be reconciled to God (Jn. 10:7).

The uniqueness of Christ is affirmed not only by Trinitarians but also by many Unitarians. The difference between the two views relates to the question of whether there is only one triune God who exists in three persons, or is there only one God, period, and one or two other spiritual entities (Jesus and the Holy Spirit) who are less than God. In my view, the line of demarcation between these two views is very fine and is mostly semantic in nature.

Now it's time to apply a bit of common sense logic to this question. Let's start by taking everything out of the picture but God Himself. Let's assume that Christ and the Holy Spirit do not yet exist. Let's also assume that the universe in which we live had not yet been created. So we start with God, and no other persons or things. All that exists is God. God is literally *"all-in-all."*

For God Himself to meaningfully exist there would have to be some context in which events and interactions, including divine thoughts, could occur in sequential order. In other words, some sort of time must exist in the mind of God. For this reason I would postulate that God is not a timeless being. He is an infinite being, but not timeless or limited in any way by the forward or reverse direction of time. He is able to experience all past, present and future events simultaneously. From God's point of view everything that ever will happen has already happened. He is able to view His creation(s) from all possible points of reference. God experiences time both sequentially and simultaneously.

I would further speculate that if God is love and loving by nature, as the Bible attests, then for any kind of loving interactions to occur there would need to be at least two or more persons or entities participating in those interactions. It would seem logical to me that God's first act in time would be the creation of one or more persons or entities with whom He could interact. According to the Bible, Christ was the first (Col. 1:15). So Christ did have a beginning in time.

Based on my knowledge of quantum mechanics and the conservation of energy (God Himself being made up of pure energy) I do not believe that Christ was created out of nothing. He was created out of or from God's own essence (pure energy). He came from God in the sense that a human baby is made from the body parts of the mother and father. Jesus was *"begotten"* from God in the same sense that human parents beget their children. Jesus was divine in the sense that everything that comes out of God is part of God Himself. He was fashioned from God's DNA, so to speak. He also had a separate and distinct personality with whom God the Father could interact.

I believe there is another reason for Christ's existence. He is the personification of a God who otherwise would be invisible, impersonal, and unknowable. *"No one has ever seen God, but the one and only Son, who is himself God and is in closest relationship with the Father, has made him known."* (John 1:18)   In other words, Christ exists for the benefit of all humanity, that we might have a way to know and connect with God, the Father.

That brings us to a discussion of the Holy Spirit, the third person of the Trinity. In the Bible God is described as being a spirit. *"God is spirit, and his worshipers must worship in the Spirit and in truth."* The same is true of Christ. He exists in Heaven today in spiritual form, in a spiritual body, not made of flesh and blood. According to 1 Cor. 15:50, *"flesh and blood cannot inherit the kingdom of God, nor does the perishable inherit the imperishable."*

In addition to being in spirit form, both God the Father and the Son have a spirit.   Christians are said to be indwelt by both the Spirit of God and the Spirit of Christ, and the two are used pretty much interchangeably. *"You, however, are not in the realm of the flesh but are in the realm of the Spirit, if indeed the Spirit of God lives in you. And if anyone does not have the Spirit of Christ, they do not belong to Christ."* (1 Cor. 3:16-18).

For me the conclusion of the matter is this. Both God the Father and Jesus Christ are different manifestations on a single divine Godhead. The term "Spirit" simply refers to "what they are made of." As God's only begotten son Christ is made up of "God parts," ie. spirit. Both the Father and Son share the same spirit, but also exist as separate entities. A very literal translation of John 1:1 expresses this connection: *"In the beginning was the Word* (ie. the Christ), *and what God was, the Word was."* Because both the Father and the Son exist in spirit form they can divide themselves into an infinite number of smaller pieces and focus their attention in many different places at once. Each piece is intimately connected with the whole and knows what all the other pieces are up to. The spirit of God can listen to millions of different prayers at the same time. God is omnipresent. His Spirit and the Spirit of Christ are everywhere. All creation is infused with the Spirit of God and of Christ. Christ is the image of the invisible God and in Christ all things hold together. *"He is the image of the invisible God, the firstborn of all creation. For by Him all things were created, both in the heavens and on earth, visible and invisible, whether thrones or dominions or rulers or authorities – all things have been created through Him and for Him. He is before all things, and in Him all things hold together."*

If you are confused by all this you are not alone. Rather than trying to figure this all out, it might be best to just go with the flow and use biblical descriptions and don't be too bothered by the ambiguities. The deeper things of God are sometimes beyond human comprehension, and may be experienced without being fully understood.

So how do we human beings fit into all this? Are you a spiritual being with a physical body, or are you a physical body that possesses a human spirit, or are you only a physical being with no spirit? According to Romans 8:16, *"The Spirit Himself testifies with our spirit that we are children of God."* Human beings do have a spirit. Another word for the human spirit is the "soul." This is indicated in the parallelism in Luke 1:46-47, *"And Mary said: 'My soul glorifies the Lord and my spirit rejoices in God my savior."* In this passage, the words "soul" and "spirit" are used interchangeably. There is a sense in which the spirit or soul refers to our real or whole self, as opposed to just the material self. In

Genesis 2:7, man is described as becoming a *"living soul"* after God breathes into him the breath of life.

Two other sources of truth also confirm the idea that man is a spiritual being, the testimony of science and the testimony of millions of people who have had near death experiences (NDE's).
As I mentioned earlier in this book many scientists, especially theoretical physicists, are coming to realize that we don't actually live in a physical, material world, but a "supernatural" world instead. Their belief in a natural world subject only to the natural laws of Newtonian physics has given way to the idea that the world we observe and experience consists solely of immaterial waves of energy that do not collapse into reality unless observed by conscious observers who themselves do not actually reside within this universe, and are in a manner of speaking spiritual rather than physical beings.

The evidence for the reality and genuineness of the out-of-body near death experience (NDE) is in my view irrefutable. The testimony of millions of people who have had near death experiences, most of whom were clinically dead at the time, confirms the fact that the spirit or soul of man exists quite independently of the physical body and survives after death.

According to the Bible our entire universe, including all the people in it, was created through Christ. Christ is the intermediary through whom God created us. But we were not created out of nothing. Life was breathed into us by the Spirit of God. So you could say that we all share a divine connection with God. Because we were created by Christ we are basically made up of "Christ parts," or spirit. We were created in the image of God, who is spirit. It is also apparent, however, that most of us are not consciously aware of this and feel isolated from God. Most of us view God as a divine being who lives up in Heaven somewhere in a separate place. Of course God Has not separated Himself from us. Instead God has literally breathed Himself into all of us and given to all of us a portion of His Spirit. The difference between those who are saved and those who are not has to do with our awareness and experience of this connection.

When Jesus actually entered into the space-time universe which He created, it was for the purpose of identifying with and communicating with His created beings, who during their time on Earth are incapable of directly communicating with God the Father or with Christ Himself, or the Holy Spirit, for that matter. The immaterial and the material have no way of making direct visible or auditory contact. They exist in two entirely separate planes of existence. We can't see, hear, or touch God with our physical senses.

When Christ took human form it was necessary for Him, in order to become fully human, to divest himself of many of His divine attributes. As an actual physical human being, He like the rest of us did not have the ability to see, touch and feel God in the way that He could before His incarnation. He started out from scratch, as it were, and had to learn who He really was and subject Himself to the limitations that all rest of us face. He was no longer omniscient because His mind was no longer connected to God in the way that it once was. He was no longer divine and He was fully human in every respect. When He said that God was greater than He, He was being truthful. He was totally dependent upon God for everything that He accomplished on Earth. He needed to pray for God's help just like the rest of us. He experienced all the human passions and temptations that the rest of us feel. When He came to Earth He literally *"emptied"* Himself of His Godhood and became a servant of God, and demonstrated God's love for us by dying on the cross of Calvary for the sins of the world (See Philippians 2:6-11). After the resurrection everything He gave up in order to fulfill His mission on Earth was restored to Him., and He was given a name that would be above all names. Every knee will eventually bow to Him and He will be worshipped as Lord by everyone. Once everyone has learned their life lessons and been formed into the likeness of Christ, they will be presented by Christ to God, faultless before God's throne (see Jude 1:24).

So is there only one God? Yes. Is Jesus God? Yes. I would say that He is a part of God and has all the attributes of God, but at the same time He has a personality that is separate and distinct from God. He is both the object of God's love and the vehicle through whom God expresses His love towards untold billions of His created beings. When on Earth was Jesus fully human? Yes. He came from God, but in His actual conscious awareness He was not God and did not, at least in the beginning, have direct knowledge of who He really was. Like the rest of us, He had to grow in wisdom and stature and favor with both God and man.

To summarize, everything that comes from God or is created by God is technically part of God. God is by nature multi-dimensional in that respect. From our point of view within the confines of the physical bodies in which we temporarily reside we are separated from God. Our personal experiences play out over time, but from God's perspective, they have already occurred and there was never a time that they did not yet occur. Christ was begotten of God, but from God's perspective there was never a time in which Christ did not exist. The Holy Spirit is just another name for God Himself and also of Christ. The Spirit of God is the same as the Spirit of Christ. It is that part of God that connects directly with our human spirit, our real self. One day Christ will gather all of us up in Himself, completely perfected, and present us to the Father, and we will experience complete oneness with God the Father, Son and Holy Spirit, and God will finally be "all in all." (See 1 Cor. 15:22-28 and Jude 1:24-25.

Chapter 9

Theological Correctness

Theological correctness refers to the insistence of many religious conservatives upon the profession of certain theological beliefs as a necessary condition of Christian salvation and inclusion in the family of God. For many Christian conservatives the Gospel of Jesus Christ is good news, it would seem, only for those who are fortunate enough to be exposed to this belief system and subscribe to it. It doesn't matter how religious, moral, or otherwise deserving an individual might be, salvation and entrance into God's heavenly kingdom is only available to those who subscribe to a very detailed system of theological beliefs about the work and person of Jesus Christ. In other words, in order to be saved one must not only be spiritually, morally and ethically correct, but theologically correct as well.

Just how detailed is this system of necessary and required beliefs? Well, in the view of many conservative Christians, it is more detailed than you might think. For example, it is not enough to be a follower of Jesus Christ and seek to obey his religious and ethical teachings. There are certain specific teachings about his person and ministry that you must also subscribe to. You must believe that He is not only the Son of God, but is uniquely the *"only begotten"* son of God and at the same time He is also God Himself. Additionally, you must believe in the atonement, and not just any definition or theory of the atonement will do. You must believe in what is referred to as the substitutionary atonement, that Jesus on the cross of Calvary took upon himself the sins of all mankind, and paid the penalty for your sins. In order to be saved you must receive Christ as your personal Savior and Lord and ask forgiveness for your sins based on Jesus shed blood on the cross of Calvary. In other words, it is not enough just to believe that Jesus is the unique son of God, and is actually God himself, the third person of the Trinity, and that He died for the sins of mankind, but you must also believe that he rose bodily from the dead and is alive today, and you must enter into a personal relationship with him and ask him to forgive your sins based on his shed blood on Calvary. And you need to be sincere about it! Hypocrites and unbelievers will definitely not be admitted into Heaven. Exactly how strong or perfect your belief or faith must be has never been made clear. Just to be sure, it would help to produce a sufficient amount of follow-through and good works as evidence that your faith is genuine.

Naturally the above level of theological correctness would pretty much rule out 99 percent of the people on earth as candidates for salvation. Most Roman Catholics wouldn't make it, because they rely mostly on their good works for salvation and have little understanding of the principle of salvation by *"grace apart from works."* Mormons are excluded because although they believe that Jesus is the Son of God they don't believe he is the unique Son of God and that He is actually God Himself. And of course, Mormons don't really believe in the Christian God, because they believe that God was once a man and that it is possible for men to actually become gods. Boy, talk about theological incorrectness! Jehovah's witnesses are excluded because they don't believe in the Trinity or that Jesus was the unique son of God, and they rely mostly on their own good works for their salvation. Many, if not most, Christian liberals are excluded because they don't believe in the deity of Christ or the resurrection of Christ or the substitutionary atonement. Even though many of those Christian liberals are deeply devoted to God and seek to follow the teachings of Christ, they are not technically born again or saved.

If most professing Christians are not theologically correct enough to enter Heaven, what chance is there for the Hindu, Moslem, Buddhist, Atheist, or the starving beggar on the streets of Calcutta who doesn't have even the slightest clue that he is loved by God.

Nevertheless, the Bible does teach that theological correctness is an important part of the salvation process. The issue I have with those who insist on theological correctness as a condition of salvation concerns the timing of it. Becoming saved and experiencing Christian salvation is a process that does not occur at any one instantaneous point in time. None of us are completely saved yet. The converse is also true. No one is completely lost. I believe that Christ made provision on Calvary for the salvation of everyone, and everyone is in the process of becoming fully saved. God is at work in our lives before, during and after our profession of theologically correct beliefs about Jesus Christ. In my view, religiously devout individuals who are genuinely seeking to please God, though misinformed on many important theological points of doctrine, may be closer to God, and farther along in the salvation process, than individuals who subscribe to all the correct doctrines but are not seeking to please God in many important aspects of their lives. Filling the gaps in our theological understanding is something that God will do for all of us sooner or later. For most, this will not occur until after death.

Experiencing Christ

As part of my research for a thesis which I wrote in college, I surveyed the beliefs of a variety of Christian denominations. I developed a doctrinal questionnaire and administered it to the entire congregations of several Christian churches. One of the questions listed several "fundamental" Christian doctrines which included the following: Belief in the Deity of Christ; the Substitutionary Atonement; the Virgin Birth of Christ; the Resurrection of Christ from the Dead; acknowledgment of Christ as Lord of one's life; repentance from sin; the literal, verbal inerrancy of the Scriptures; and a few others. The question was, *"Which of the items on the list are absolutely necessary for salvation?"* As one might expect, members of the more liberal denominations checked fewer items on the list than members of the more conservative denominations. Many members of very conservative fundamentalist congregations checked every single item on the list.

The conditions for salvation are further complicated by the difficulty of establishing exactly how much belief or faith would be required. Belief, or faith, is characterized in many Bible passages as being strong or weak in various circumstances and from one individual to the next. How would one distinguish between saving faith and faith which doesn't quite cut it? This is not an easy question to answer.

In the case of the prerequisite of repentance from sin and acknowledging Jesus Christ as Lord of one's life, how is it possible to know for sure just how much repentance is required or to what degree a person must yield to the Lordship of Christ in his or her life?

The problem resolves itself, however, if you define a Christian to be a person who has a personal relationship with Christ, rather than a person who merely subscribes to a system of beliefs. As you know after reading this far into this book, I believe that everyone is in the process of becoming saved. I believe that one day all creation will become fully reconciled to Christ. I believe that Christ died for the benefit of all mankind, and because of this all mankind will eventually become saved.

Most Christians would agree with the Apostle Paul that we are saved by grace, not works. We come to Christ "as we are" with all of our sinful baggage and with woefully inadequate faith and doctrinal understanding. He turns none of us away (see John 6:37). He loves every one of us with infinite, *"agape,"* love and sees us not only as we are, but also as we will become.

Our salvation is *"in Christ"* (see Rom. 3:24; 8:1; 1 Cor. 1:30; 15:22; 2 Cor. 5:19; 2 Tim. 1:1; 2:10). What that means is that our salvation is in our relationship with Christ. The degree to which we experience Christ in our lives is the degree to which we have become saved. The Gospel of Christ is good news. It is not a set of intellectual, doctrinal, and behavioral barriers which we must overcome in order to be accepted by God.

By regarding Christian salvation as something one experiences, rather than something one acquires at a specific point in time, most of the difficult doctrinal issues resolve themselves. One no longer needs to wonder, "Am I saved or not?" The religious elite of Jesus' day were harshly criticized by Christ for their hypocritical and self-righteous attitudes. On the other hand, Jesus was welcoming and kind to those who were regarded by the religious elite as the least worthy, such as the woman caught in adultery, the poor widow who only had one small coin to donate, the tax collector, the despised Samaritan, the Roman Centurion, lepers, outcasts of society, and especially children who knew little or nothing about religious doctrine.

No one ever got saved by knowing or believing something about God (see James, Chapter 2). We experience God's salvation only as we experience Christ himself. Some view the salvation experience as inviting Christ to forgive your sins and asking Christ to come and live inside your heart. If that's as far as it ever goes, however, it cannot be said that you have become fully saved. You may have taken a very important first step, but you may only be regarded as a *"babe in Christ"* (see 1 Cor. 3:1). If you invite Christ into your life, but don't allow Him to control various aspects of your life, then He is not really living inside you. Christ is omnipresent. Technically He lives everywhere. He exists inside and outside of everyone. When the Bible refers to Christ as abiding or living inside of you, it is not talking about Christ merely taking up space. When Paul said, *"for to me to live is Christ" (Phil. 1:21),* he was saying that he was allowing Jesus to control every aspect of his life. Paul yielded up his body, his hands, his feet, his mind, and allowed Christ to use them as instruments for carrying out the ministry of spreading the gospel. Paul so completely identified with Christ that he could honestly say, *"I no longer live, but Christ lives in me" (Gal. 2:20)*

So, exactly how does one go about experiencing Christ, as described above? The key to achieving this is to focus on the relationship with Christ and not on acts of obedience and the avoidance of sin. God loves and accepts you just as you are. There

77

is nothing you can do to be worthy of God's love or in any way be deserving of the salvation He offers to you in Christ. Salvation is a gift that God offers to all. There are no preconditions that must be met. All that remains for you to do is to experience it. All you need to do is allow Christ into your life and get to know Him. Thank Him for everything He has done for you and ask for His help and guidance with every important decision you need to make in life. Share with Him all your burdens, heartaches, disappointments, worries and cares. Ask Him to intercede in your life and the lives of those whom you love and those whom you ought to love. Ask Him to help you develop qualities of Godly character and experience the fruit of the Spirit, such as love, joy, peace, patience, kindness, goodness, faithfulness, gentleness and self-control. When you stumble, ask Him to pick you up. When you think wrong thoughts or act in selfish ways or commit wrongful acts, ask Him to forgive you. Ask Him to forgive you for sins which you are not yet willing to give up. It's OK. He understands. Rome wasn't built in a day. Your salvation experience is an ages-long journey that begins with just a few halting steps.

Paul admonishes us to *"pray without ceasing"* (1 Thes. 5:17). Talk to God throughout the day, every day. In the beginning you may only remember to talk with Him once or twice a day, or once or twice a week. That's OK. He is always by your side anyway. He will never leave you nor forsake you. It's hard to discipline yourself to spend hours on your knees each day in fervent prayer, as is the habit of some (not many). I myself prefer a more casual approach. Brother Lawrence, a medieval monk, described his experience with Christ as *"practicing the presence of God."* It was simply a matter of continually reminding himself that God was present in his life and cared about every daily activity of life. Brother Lawrence played a very humble role in the monastery. He worked mostly in the kitchen and referred to God as *"the God of the pots and pans."* Even in the most mundane aspects of daily living, Brother Lawrence enjoyed the presence of God.

God's perfect standards of behavior are impossible for anyone to attain in this life. You will never measure up to those standards.

The harder you try to please God by measuring up to those impossible standards the more defeated and frustrated you will become in your daily walk with Christ. Most likely, you will give up trying altogether. The secret to making progress in your Christian walk is to not try so hard. Keep the lines of communication open between Christ and yourself. Transfer the load onto the back of Christ and allow him to carry it for you (see Matt. 11:28-29). He wants to live His life through you. When you transfer the burdens of daily living and Christian service to Him, then it becomes His problem and not yours. He is more than capable of doing what you cannot possibly do in your own strength.

Is it really that easy, you might ask? What about passages in the Bible that indicate the necessity of self-denial and sacrifice as a condition of salvation and following Christ? Did not Christ say that if you did not love Him even more than your own family you were not worthy of Him? Did He not say that in order to follow Him you would have to deny yourself, take up a cross of suffering daily? Did He not say that if your righteousness did not exceed that of the Scribes and Pharisees you could not enter the Kingdom of Heaven? Did He not say that you cannot serve two masters and that you had to choose between serving the "world" and serving Him? Did not the Apostle Paul say in Romans that a true Christian is one who has yielded himself to Christ as an obedient servant?

Here's my answer. In response to one of those harsh sayings of Jesus, his disciples asked, *"How then can anyone be saved?"* Jesus answer was that with God all things are possible (see Matt. 19:16-27). The process of becoming a Christian and becoming saved is not instantaneous. A Chinese philosopher once said that a journey of a thousand miles begins with a single step. The salvation process involves identifying with Christ and getting to know Him on a more and more personal level as time goes on. Apart from Christ we can accomplish nothing of lasting value (John 15:5). The Christian walk is characterized as a process of letting go, rather than trying harder. It involves stepping aside and allowing Christ to step in. Salvation is a gift, not a result of good works. There is no room for boasting. Christian baptism pictures our salvation as a process of identifying with Christ in His death, burial and resurrection. We die to our old way of life and rise up with Christ in newness of life. We shed the old and put on the new. In the words of Paul, *"old things pass away and all things become new"* (2 Cor. 5:17). The key to all this is our relationship with and our identification with Christ. Our salvation is *"in Christ."* We are only saved to the extent that we abide in Christ.

One day we will become completely saved, and our final redemption will result not from our own efforts but from the work of Christ in our hearts and minds. It is He who is able to keep us safe until that day and eventually present us faultless before the throne of God (Jude 1:24). So, relax, and quit worrying about not being able to measure up. Practice the presence of Christ in your life with every step you take. Be aware of His presence and closeness to you. Bring every care and concern to Him and ask Him to handle it for you. Ask Him for His strength to carry on when faced with difficult, even impossible circumstances. Thank Him continually for the bountiful blessings in your life. The closer you walk with Christ, the more like Him you will become. The more you experience Christ Himself, the more you will experience the fruit of His Spirit in your life. This fruit includes not only the benefits of love, joy, and peace, but also the development of Godly character, which includes traits such as patience, kindness, goodness, faithfulness, gentleness and self- control.

Self-denial is a part of that package, but what you receive in return makes everything else pale by comparison. If you want your dog to let go of the dirty old bone he dug up in the back yard present him with a nice juicy steak. That is what God does for you. He wants you to give up your old way of life, but the new life He gives you in return is infinitely better than the one you are leaving behind.

The Importance of Knowing God by the Name Jesus

We need to keep in mind that God the Father and Jesus Christ are in a very real sense one and the same. Jesus is the means by which an unknowable God makes Himself known here on earth. When we pray to Jesus, we are at the same time praying to God. When we address God as our Heavenly Father, we are also addressing Jesus Christ. When we ask for guidance of the Holy Spirit, we are talking to both the Spirit of God and the Spirit of Christ. In the Bible they are used interchangeably. Try not to get too hung on the name, Jesus. Yes, there is something wonderful about that name. But, we don't worship a name. We worship the person behind that name. Jesus was the name given to God incarnate during His earthly sojourn. Who really knows what name He went by in the heavenly realms before His incarnation? Who really knows what name He goes by today in the heavenly realms? We know from the Near Death Accounts (NDEs), that in Heaven communication is telepathic and no actual words are involved. People are recognized in ways that do not involve physical names. When the Bible says that Jesus has been given a name which is above every name and that at the name of Jesus every knee will bow, I believe the reference is to the person behind the name, not the name itself.

Why do I say all this? The reason is that many devoutly religious people of other faiths, who do not know God by the name Jesus, are not excluded from the salvation that God freely offers to all. Jesus listens to their prayers, just as He listens to ours. You might believe that not addressing Jesus by name is theologically incorrect. In my view, that is an error that can be easily corrected later in this life or in the next. God is at work in all of our lives before, during, and after our profession of faith in Jesus Christ.

Chapter 10

Popular Misconceptions about Hell

For most of my life I have been perplexed and, frankly, stumped by apparent incongruities in the Bible concerning the nature of God, especially the BIG question that we have all asked ourselves. How can a God of love send the majority of the human race to eternal torment in Hell, most of whom are really pretty decent folks, at least by human standards? Most Christians struggle with this question, and the answers most of us have come up with are not all that satisfying. This is probably the single greatest theological issue confronting most Christians today.

Although most Christians are greatly disturbed by the doctrine of Hell, there is no avoiding the issue, as the concept of Hell is derived from the New Testament, with some of the most disturbing passages coming from the lips of Christ Himself. Hell is pictured by most Christians as a place of everlasting torment, and the imagery most commonly used is that of a fiery judgment, from which there is no escape.

In general, Christians are among the kindest, most forgiving and loving people on the planet, so the doctrine of Hell is not something they are comfortable with. As a result, this doctrine is reluctantly accepted, but almost never mentioned from the pulpits or in the Sunday Schools and Bible studies. In the healthiest and fastest-growing congregations the emphasis is placed on the positive aspects of the Gospel and on issues related to successful Christian living.

In an effort to mitigate the negative aspects of this teaching many Christians tend to rationalize to some extent and interpret the "flames" as symbolic of some sort of mental, rather than physical, torture. It also helps some to know that people who go to Hell will be there as a result of their own choices in life. Although very few people would deliberately choose to go to Hell, they nevertheless choose Hell by default when they decide not to follow Christ. Another mitigating factor would be the fact that there apparently are "degrees" of punishment in Hell, just as there are degrees of reward in Heaven. There are a few passages in the New Testament that seem to support this (See Matt. 11:20-22; 2 Cor. 9:6; 5:9-10). And on the positive side, the gift of God is eternal life. One should be grateful that any are saved at all, since all are sinners and the wages of sin is death,* according to Romans 6:23. *(*In many Christian circles the "death" penalty for sin is equated with eternal banishment to Hell.)*

Many Christians, despite the above mitigating facts, are very uncomfortable with the notion of Hell and prefer not to think about it. Although most Christians believe in Hell with their intellects, it appears that they don't really believe in it with their hearts. In other words, they act as though they don't believe in it. Most are only mildly disturbed that many of their friends and neighbors, not to mention close family members or relatives, might be headed to Hell after they die.

The situation is further exacerbated by the fact that the life-saving Gospel message does not reach everyone and some are predisposed not to believe it because of very strong religious and cultural biases against Christianity. Not all Christians believe this. Some have a more "inclusive" theology and believe that it is possible for non-Christians to become saved without hearing the Gospel message, under certain circumstances, which are not very clearly understood or articulated.

The Bible does teach that by the end of the ages, every knee will bow to Christ and every tongue will confess Him as Lord. At the same time, the Bible also teaches that before that happens many of us will be experiencing "hells" of our own making. There is a huge difference, in my view, however, between the popular view of Hell and what actually happens after death.

The popular view of Hell is based on several misconceptions:

The first misconception about Hell is that punishment in Hell lasts forever. Most people assume that the words "everlasting" and "eternal" are accurate translations of the original Hebrew and Greek words in the Bible. Actually, there is no word in Greek or Hebrew that means everlasting or never ending in the sense that most of us understand it. The words which are translated as *"eternal," "everlasting,"* and *"forever"* are all variants of the Hebrew word *"olam"* and its New Testament Greek counterpart *"aion."* Sometimes the singular version is used; sometimes the plural, and sometimes the adjective. In each case, the reference is to a period of time with a definite beginning and end, which is the exact opposite of the meaning of "eternal" and "everlasting." Sometimes phrases like *"into the ages"* or *"the ages of the ages"* are used to denote several distinct epochs or periods of time in succession to one another. It could be argued that the writers of the Bible, although they had no word for "unending," still intended that meaning. However, the words do not have to be interpreted that way. They can also be interpreted to mean exactly what they meant in the Greek and Hebrew culture, with each age having a beginning and an end. This would be consistent with the New and Old Testament teaching that eventually, after time as we know it comes to an end, and the "ages" come to an end, God will "reconcile" all creation, including all created beings, to Christ. (See 1 Cor. 15:22-28)

The most common argument against this line of reasoning is that if the Greek words which are mistranslated as "eternal" don't really mean "unending" with respect to Hell, wouldn't that mean that they also don't meant "eternal" when used to describe eternal life in Christ? My answer to that question is, yes, you would be exactly right about that. *"Aionian"* life, often mistranslated *"eternal"* life, does not refer to the "duration," but instead to the quality of our life in Christ. The Greek term *"Aionian"* literally means belonging to or pertaining to an age or ages. It means exactly the opposite of eternal and everlasting. Nowhere in the Bible does it refer to an infinite, unending period of time. When Jesus gives us *aionian* life, the life He gives us is Himself. He is the *"way, the truth, and the life."* Everyone will live eternally, both Christians and non-Christians alike. All people continue to live after death in the sense that their conscious existence will never come to an end. *Aionian* life does not refer to never ending conscious existence. Even those who believe in everlasting punishments of the wicked in Hell will acknowledge that the wicked possess everlasting conscious existence. Instead, *aionian* life refers to our quality of existence IN CHRIST (See Rom: 3:24; 6:3-4; 8:1-2, 1-11; 1 Cor. 1:30; 2 Cor. 5:17; 15:22; Eph. 1:1-9; Col. 3:4; 2 Tim. 1:1; 2:19).

If *aionian* life referred to the length of our life the meaning of the phrase would be completely lost. The emphasis should not be placed on the word *aionian*, but instead on the word "life." What distinguishes the Christian from the non-Christian is not the length of his life, but the nature of it. Bible passages which refer to *aionian* life are referring to spiritual life vs. spiritual death, not physical life and death. As Christians, we experience spiritual life in our present walk in this world and during the eons, or ages, to come. To have *aionian* life is to be alive spiritually in Christ. Those who do not have *aionian* life are dead spiritually and separated from Christ in this life, a condition which sometimes, but not always, continues after death. Technically Christ still resides within all of us, but not all are consciously aware of this and as a result are not able to experience *"aionian"* life.

A second misconception about Hell is that the purpose of God's judgments (ie. the "hells" of our own making) on the unsaved are retribution for the sins they have committed. The purpose of God's chastisement is not retribution, but correction. Although we are all in the process of being saved, we still remain subject to the temporal consequences of our sinful behavior in this world and sometimes the next. Because He loves us, we often find ourselves on the receiving end of God's "tough love." To a great extent God has created a self-adjusting universe. The judgments of our Lord do not usually come directly from His hand. They mostly result from the natural laws which He has set in motion, by which *we "reap what we sow."* (See Galatians 6:7) This has the purpose of teaching us valuable life lessons, bringing us to repentance, and restoring us to a loving relationship with Himself through Christ.

A third misconception about Hell is that it is a place of physical torture and torment for everyone there. Although many New Testament passages teach that there will be suffering in Hell, not all will suffer in the same degree. It is conceivable that for some the punishments (ie. God's corrective actions) will be relatively mild when compared to the fate of others. The Hebrew justice system was based on fairness, and the punishments fit the crimes exactly, as specified in Leviticus 24:19-21: *"Anyone who injures their neighbor is to be injured in the same manner: fracture for fracture, eye for eye, tooth for tooth. The one who has inflicted the injury must suffer the same injury."*

In Matthew 5:38-48, Jesus took this law of reciprocity to a whole new level by asking us to return good for evil. *"You have heard that it was said, 'Eye for eye, and tooth for tooth.' But I tell you, do not resist an evil person. If anyone slaps you on the right cheek, turn to them the other cheek also. And if anyone wants to sue you and take your shirt, hand over your coat as well. If anyone forces you to go one mile, go with them two miles. Give to the one who asks you, and do not turn away from the one who wants to borrow from you. You have heard that it was said, 'Love your neighbor and hate your enemy.' But I tell you, love your enemies and pray for those who persecute you, that you may be children of your Father in heaven. He causes his sun to rise on the evil and the good, and sends rain on the righteous and the unrighteous. If you love those who love you, what reward will you get? Are not even the tax collectors doing that? And if you greet only your own people, what are you doing more than others? Do not even pagans do that? Be perfect, therefore, as your heavenly Father is perfect."*

Not only is God's justice fair and equitable, with punishments fitting the crimes, but it also includes mercy and forgiveness. Jesus asks us to forgive our enemies so that we might become perfect as God is perfect. In other words, it is the character of God to be loving and forgiving. God's punishments are not disproportionate to the crimes. He doesn't punish temporal sins with infinite punishment in a place called Hell. He doesn't ask us to forgive our enemies, while at the same time refusing to do the same Himself. That would make God the biggest hypocrite of all time.

A fourth misconception about Hell is that the imagery of fire is symbolic of torture and excruciating pain. While most Christians believe that the fires of Hell are not literal, they still believe they symbolize extreme suffering, torment and regret. In my view this is only partially true. While a certain amount of pain and regret would be involved in most disciplinary actions, the result is a good one. According to Hebrews 12:11, *"No discipline seems pleasant at the time, but painful. Later on, however, it produces a harvest of righteousness and peace for those who have been trained by it."*

Throughout the Bible the imagery of fire is symbolic of cleansing and purification, not torture. The fires of God's judgment will not be pleasant to endure. Nevertheless, the result will be repentance and purification. According to the prophet Zephaniah, after God's fiery judgment ALL will *"call on the name of the LORD and serve him shoulder to shoulder."*

Zephaniah 3:8-9: *"Therefore wait for me,' declares the LORD, 'for the day I will stand up to testify. I have decided to assemble the nations, to gather the kingdoms and to pour out my wrath on them—all my fierce anger. The whole world will be consumed by the fire of my jealous anger. Then will I purify the lips of the peoples, that all of them may call on the name of the LORD and serve him shoulder to shoulder."*

The prophet Malachi uses the imagery of a refiner's fire or a launderer's soap to describe the day in which the Messiah will bring judgment on Israel.

Malachi 3:1-4: *"See, I will send my messenger, who will prepare the way before me. Then suddenly the Lord you are seeking will come to his temple; the messenger of the covenant, whom you desire, will come," says the LORD Almighty. But who can endure the day of his coming? Who can stand when he appears? For he will be like a refiner's fire or a launderer's soap. He will sit as a refiner and purifier of silver; he will purify the Levites and refine them like gold and silver. Then the LORD will have men who will bring offerings in righteousness, and the offerings of Judah and Jerusalem will be acceptable to the LORD, as in days gone by, as in former years."*

In the above passage fire is used as an instrument of cleansing and purification, and the Levites are refined like gold and silver. In other words, they are purged of their sins and made righteous. This interpretation is in accordance with the New Testament teaching that none of us are righteous and all are in need of cleansing and forgiveness.

In Matthew 3:10-12, John the Baptist, the *"Messenger"* mentioned in the above quote from Malachi, uses the same imagery. *"The ax is already at the root of the trees, and every tree that does not produce good fruit will be cut down and thrown into the fire. I baptize you with water for repentance. But after me will come one who is more powerful than I, whose sandals I am not fit to carry. He will baptize you with the Holy Spirit and with fire. His winnowing fork is in his hand, and he will clear his threshing floor, gathering his wheat into the barn and burning up the chaff with unquenchable fire."*

The above passage can be interpreted two ways. The first interpretation is that Jesus will baptize Christians with both the Holy Spirit and with fire. The second interpretation is that Jesus will baptize the Christians with the Holy Spirit and non-Christians with fire. The latter view better fits the context in which John likens this process as one of separating the wheat from the chaff and burning up the chaff with unquenchable fire. It doesn't matter which position you take on this, however, the imagery is still consistent with Malachi's depiction of the fires of God's judgment as a refining process.

According to the Apostle Paul in 1 Cor. 3:11-15, even Christians will experience the refining fires of God's judgment, though perhaps to a lesser degree. *"For no one can lay any foundation other than the one already laid, which is Jesus Christ. If anyone builds on this foundation using gold, silver, costly stones, wood, hay or straw, their work will be shown for what it is, because the Day will bring it to light. It will be revealed with fire, and the fire will test the quality of each person's work. If what has been built survives, the builder will receive a reward. If it is burned up, the builder will suffer loss but yet will be saved—even though only as one escaping through the flames."*

A fifth misconception about Hell is that only God's elect or chosen ones may avoid it. Many students of the Bible believe that the purpose of our election is that God has chosen or elected or chose us for salvation, and everyone else was chosen for eternal damnation. This is the same mistake that the Hebrew nation made in Old Testament times. They assumed that they were a nation chosen by God for special favor and privilege, when in reality they were chosen for service and were supposed to be a light to the Gentiles and were to become the vehicle through whom God would bless all nations. We Christians are a royal priesthood chosen by God to be a light to the unsaved and reach them for Christ. If God truly is sovereign over His creation and desires that all men be saved, then He is perfectly capable of achieving that end. We Christians must regard ourselves as among the first fruits of God's plan of redemption. We are not privileged, to the exclusion of all others. Instead, we are privileged to be used by God to spread the Gospel to all nations.

The passage of Scripture most often used by Hyper-Calvinists to support their doctrine of double predestination is Romans, Chapters 9-11. Double predestination is the teaching that God predestines only a chosen few, the elect, for salvation, and by default He predestines everyone else to spend eternity in Hell. In this Scripture passage the Apostle Paul teaches exactly the opposite. Here is the sequence of events as Paul describes them in Romans 9-11:

In Romans 9, Paul explains that our salvation is based on God's mercy and not on man's desire or effort. It's completely up to God who gets saved and who remains unsaved (ie. whose hearts are hardened). God hardened Pharoah's heart for the benefit of releasing the Hebrew nation, His chosen people, from slavery and displaying His power in the process.

Romans 9:16-18, *"It does not, therefore, depend on man's desire or effort, but on God's mercy. For the Scripture says to Pharaoh: 'I raised you up for this very purpose, that I might display my power in you and that my name might be proclaimed in all the earth.' Therefore God has mercy on whom he wants to have mercy, and he hardens whom he wants to harden."*

Later in the same chapter Paul explains that it was God's plan to eventually save both Jews and Gentiles. The Gentiles, who were not originally God's chosen people, would one day also be called God's people.

Romans 9:23-24, *"He did this to make the riches of his glory known to the objects of his mercy, even us, whom he also called, not only from the Jews but also from the Gentiles? As he says in Hosea: 'I will call them my people who are not my people; and I will call her my loved one who is not my loved one."*

In Romans 11, Paul explains that only a remnant of the nation of Israel were elected to receive Christ, and the others were hardened.

Romans 11:7-8, *"What then? What Israel sought so earnestly it did not obtain, but the elect did. The others were hardened, as it is written: 'God gave them a spirit of stupor, eyes so that they could not see and ears so that they could not hear, to this very day.'"*

Paul then explains that the nation of Israel did not fall beyond recovery. The transgression of the nation of Israel was the occasion of the Gospel being spread to the Gentiles. He then explains that if the Israel's loss resulted in "riches for the Gentiles" how much greater will be the riches of the nation of Israel when they themselves are restored to *"fullness."*

Romans 11:11-12, *"Again I ask: Did they stumble so as to fall beyond recovery? Not at all! Rather, because of their transgression, salvation has come to the Gentiles to make Israel envious. But if their transgression means riches for the world, and their loss means riches for the gentiles, how much greater riches will their fullness bring!"*

Then Paul tells us that Israel has experienced a hardening only until a full number of the Gentiles have come in. After that, all Israel will be saved.

Romans 11:25-26, *"I do not want you to be ignorant of this mystery, brothers, so that you may not be conceited: Israel has experienced a hardening in part until the full number of the Gentiles has come in. And so all Israel will be saved, as it is written: 'The deliverer will come from Zion; he will turn godlessness away from Jacob. And this is my covenant with them when I take away their sins.'"*

Finally, at the end of Romans 11, Paul sums up the whole matter and drives the message home. He points out that just as we have received mercy as a result of the disobedience of Israel, they will receive mercy as a result of God's mercy to us. God has *"bound all men over to disobedience in order that He may have mercy on all."*

Romans 11:31-32, *"so they too have now become disobedient in order that they too may now receive mercy as a result of God's mercy to you. For God has bound ALL men over to disobedience so that he may have mercy on them ALL."* (The caps are mine)

There is no question in my mind that the Apostle Paul was a universalist.

A sixth misconception about Hell is that it is a physical place or locality. In the Old Testament the word that used to be translated "Hell" is *"Sheol,"* the place of the dead. Most modern translations do not use the word "Hell." The literal meaning is simply "unseen." It was not described as a place of suffering and torment. It was a place where everyone went after death and nothing went on there at all. It was just another word for the "grave." If anything did go on there, there was no way of knowing what it was, hence the name "unseen." The ancient Israelites did not believe in life after death. Their views are summarized in Ecclesiastes 9:5-6, *"For the living know that they will die, but the dead know nothing; they have no further reward, and even the memory of them is forgotten, their love, their hate and their jealousy have long since vanished; never again will they have a part in anything that happens under the sun."*

During the Babylonian Captivity the Jews were introduced to the concept of a dualistic conflict between God and Satan, and the additional concepts of rewards and punishments after death in Heaven or Hell. These were taken from the religions of the Babylonians (Mesopotamian myths) and the Persians (Zoroastrianism) during the Captivity. During that period the concept of Satan found its way into the Old Testament, much of which was written during the Babylonian Captivity and thereafter, including the story of Adam and Eve in the Garden of Eden. During the 400-year period between the captivity and the time of Christ, after returning to Palestine, Jewish theology was also influenced by the Greeks, who were in turn had been influenced by the Egyptians, and the doctrine of Hell developed into what is now pictured in some of the apocalyptic and apocryphal literature of the intertestamental period, and eventually found its way into the New Testament as well, particularly in the Book of Revelation. In the New Testament the *"Sheol"* of the Old Testament was transliterated into the Greek word *"Hades,"* which was the "underworld" of Greek mythology.

If you want to believe in this version of Hell you must also believe that it is either an unseen place where nothing at all happens, or a fiery place somewhere under or near the center of the Earth where people are tortured in literal flames. Take your pick.

The other word for Hell in the New Testament is *"Gehenna,"* the garbage dump outside Jerusalem in the Valley of the Son of Hinnom, where in ages past babies were sacrificed to the Canaanite God Molek. In Jesus' day this place was used to burn the garbage from the city and was continually ablaze, and it was full of disgusting worms. Today the garbage dump is gone and I understand that it is quite nice there now, especially in the Spring. In the Synoptic Gospels (Matthew, Mark, and Luke) Gehenna was the word used most often by Jesus, actually eleven times, to describe the fate of those who were not ready for the Kingdom. In the parable of the rich man and poor man, Jesus used the word *"hades."*

Not many evangelicals believe that Hell it is a place of literal fire and torment. Most of them believe that the flames are a metaphor for suffering. I quite agree with this interpretation. I would expand the meaning to include purification as well, as in the case of a crucible or furnace in which gold ore is refined into pure gold. Jesus made frequent use of parables and metaphors to illustrate underlying truths. He used the terms *"Gehenna"* and *"Hades"* because they were well-known and commonly used in the popular culture. I seriously doubt that *"Gehenna"* and *"Hades"* refer to a literal places where people go after they die. Even if this were true there is no reason to assume that the flames are literal or that people will be trapped there for all eternity, without any chance of escape. There is absolutely no Scriptural support for that.

If *"Sheol"* or Hell is a literal fiery place, then the event described in Revelation 20:13-15 makes no sense at all. *"And the sea gave up the dead which were in it, and death and Hades gave up the dead which were in them; and they were judged, every one of them according to their deeds. Then death and Hades were thrown into the lake of fire. This is the second death, the lake of fire. And if anyone's name was not found written in the book of life, he was thrown into the lake of fire."* What would be the point of throwing Hell into Hell? If the Lake of Fire is the second death why throw death into it? Two negatives make a positive. If death and Hell were destroyed, wouldn't the result be the elimination of both? If we rightly assume that death and the fires of Hades are metaphors for God's corrective judgments on sinners, and spiritual separation from God, then destroying them in the Lake of Fire would be a good thing, not a bad thing. Destroying death would make everyone alive. The second death is just the opposite of physical or spiritual death. It actually refers to the elimination of both. It is the "death of death," so to speak. Even Satan was thrown into the Lake of Fire (Rev.20:10), symbolizing the fact that even he will be cleansed and purified in the fires of God's righteous judgments. According to 1 Corinthians 15:26, *"The last enemy to be destroyed is death."* Just a few verses earlier (v. 22), the Apostle Paul pointed that *"as in Adam ALL die, so in Christ ALL will be made alive."* (the caps are mine)

Finally if all sinners at the end of the ages are literally thrown into a Lake of Fire *"for ever and ever,"* prior to the creation of the New Heavens and New Earth, why are all those sinners still hanging around outside the gates of the New Jerusalem? See Rev. 22:14, *"Blessed are those who wash their robes, that they may have the right to the tree of life and may go through the gates into the city. Outside are the dogs, those who practice magic arts, the sexually immoral, the murderers, the idolaters and everyone who loves and practices falsehood."*

The chronology and imagery of the Book Revelation were never meant to be taken literally. The whole thing was a dream or vision, after all. If you try to make literal sense out of it, all you end up with are absurdities.

Chapter 11

Predestination and Free Will

Calvinism

Years ago, when I was first exposed to an extreme form of Calvinism, I was shocked to learn that the doctrine of predestination was still alive and well. It hadn't died out in the era of Jonathan Edwards as I had thought. The idea that God would arbitrarily decide in advance who would be saved and who would spend eternity in Hell, without giving anyone a say in the matter, simply repulsed me. Not only was this doctrine alive and well, but it was, and still is, the predominant view in many mainline protestant denominations and even in the Baptist church, of which I was a member.

According to an extreme form of this system of thought, sometimes called hyper-Calvinism, Jesus only died for the Elect (limited atonement), and God only loves the Elect, and it is impossible to become saved by one's own volition, because God decides in advance who is going to desire to be saved and who is not. When God calls you to be saved His grace is irresistible. If He does not call you then it would be impossible for you to come to repentance and be saved. The idea is that man is totally depraved and unless God intervenes and awakens in him a desire to become saved, the result is a hardened heart that cannot be changed.

One of the main themes of this system of thought is the sovereignty of God. The idea is that God is all-powerful and completely sovereign over His creation and will absolutely accomplish all that He sets out to do. Because God is sovereign and does not save everyone, it must be assumed that God does not want everyone to be saved. Not all Calvinists are this extreme in their beliefs. Many do not believe in the limited atonement and many believe that God really does love everyone. He just loves the elect in a different way than those who are not of the elect.

All Calvinists teach that human freedom is an illusion. It only seems real because God allows us to make our own choices in life, sometimes referred to as free-agency, to distinguish it from free-will. The idea is that we are free to do what we want, but what we want is not determined by us, but by God. So we don't really possess free-will, only free-agency.

Of course, there are many Scriptures that refute these teachings, but there is also much Scriptural support for some of them.

Arminianism

Arminianism came about as a reaction against Calvinism. Arminians believe that Jesus did indeed die for everyone and that we are all genuinely free to make our own choices in life. While it is true that God decides in advance (elects, chooses, predestinates) who will become saved, His choices are based on His foreknowledge of who would be predisposed to receive the Gospel and who would not. According to Arminianism, human freedom is real and God's grace is offered freely to all.

The Arminian arguments seem sound enough at first glance, and there is much Scriptural support for this system of thought. However, as I pondered their arguments I came to a very disturbing realization. Human freedom must be an illusion, even if the Arminians are right and the Calvinists are wrong. If God doesn't determine our desire to be saved or not, what does? Can any of our choices in life actually be self-caused? While it is true that we are free to make our own choices in life, we are not free to determine what our desires will be. All of our thoughts have an antecedent cause. The choices we desire to make in life, if not directly determined by God, are at least indirectly determined by Him. After all, it was God who created the universe and set in motion random processes which resulted in our birth, genetic, social, societal, and psychological make-up and environment. We didn't choose where we would be born or in what kind of family or social environment we would be raised. All of these factors combine to make each one of us unique and different.

The reason my choices in life are different from yours is that I am different from you. Did I cause myself to be different? Not really. So, whether you believe that your uniqueness was caused by God or by random processes, it is still not self-caused. If you choose to become saved and I do not, who is to blame? Ultimately, we must "blame" God for all the choices we make in life. God is the one who started it all, knowing full-well what the result would be and how each individual life would be affected.

So, it doesn't matter whether you take the Calvinist position or the Arminian position, God is still ultimately responsible for all that happens.

Freedom of Will vs. Freedom of Choice

I do agree with the Calvinistic teaching that man does not possess free will and that God is truly sovereign over His creation, and that all human events are caused by God in accordance with His perfect will.

There are two main reasons why most people resist this teaching.

First, they resist it because they believe that God is both loving and just, and they don't think God should be blamed for unjustly condemning the majority of the human race to an everlasting Hell.

Secondly, they resist it because they don't clearly understand the difference between Freedom of Will (Free Will) and Freedom of Choice (Free Agency). Clearly, God allows us to make our own religious and moral decisions. Not only are we given this freedom of choice, but we are indeed held accountable by God for our choices. We are punished for making the wrong choices and rewarded for making the right choices.

At first glance that all seems quite fair. A serious problem arises, however, when we delve a bit deeper and ask the question, "Why do we make these choices?" Why does one individual freely choose to become saved and another individual freely choose otherwise? What is it that makes the one individual different from the other in that respect?

Some would answer in this way. An individual chooses to become saved because he desires or wants or wills to be saved. In other words, our moral and spiritual choices in life are based on what we desire, want, or will to do.

We are free to make whatever moral and spiritual choices in life that we desire to make. The Calvinist would refer to this freedom of choice as Free Agency in order to distinguish it from Free Will, which would be the freedom to choose what our desires would be in the first place. The Calvinist would agree that God allows us to freely choose to do good or evil. At the same time, however, they would argue that we do not possess free will. In other words, we do not freely choose our wants and desires.

Let me illustrate this in another way. My wife likes broccoli and I don't. We both may freely choose to eat it or not. But we don't choose whether or not we like the taste of it or would desire to eat it. If God were to perform a miracle (and indeed that would be quite a miracle) and cause me to like the taste of broccoli, then I would most certainly freely choose to eat it. If God did not perform this miracle, then I most certainly would freely choose not to eat it. So you see, it is very easy for God to influence the choices we make in life by altering the conditions of our lives which determine our attitudes and motivations.

Free will is not a Biblical term. Although the Bible clearly teaches that we are to be held accountable for the choices we make, it nowhere teaches that we made ourselves. We were all created

0009084 4020

Sell your books at
World of Books!
Go to sell.worldofbooks.com
and get an instant price
quote. We even pay the
shipping - see what your old
books are worth today!

unique and different. We did not choose our parents or our physical, mental and emotional capacities. We did not choose the bewildering variety of human events which have uniquely shaped our thought processes. Our wants and desires (our "wills") have been uniquely shaped, predetermined if you will, by our DNA and the various external events and circumstances of our existence. None of us has freely chosen who we are. We did not freely choose our own uniqueness.

It could be argued, correctly in my view, that God did not directly cause us to accept or reject His offer of salvation. It could also be correctly argued that God is indirectly the cause of everything. He created the universe and everything in it and set in motion a sequence of events that resulted in your existence and everything that is unique about you. Most would agree that when God set in motion this chain of events He foreknew what the result would be. He knew in advance what your choices would be. Apparently He was OK with this result, or He most certainly would have changed it. God is omnipotent and completely sovereign over His creation. He is more than capable of changing the outcome of all human events, should He so desire.

According to Ephesians 2:8-9, we have been saved by grace. Our salvation is *"a gift of God, not of ourselves, lest anyone should boast."* Because our salvation is not a result of anything meritorious on our part, the converse must also be true, that those who are lost remain so due to no fault of their own. Both conditions are the result of God's choice.

It has been argued that Universalism must be false because for God to eventually save everyone He would have to violate their free will and force them to receive Christ against their wills. It makes better sense that God would save only those who want to be saved, and allow others to freely choose not to be saved.

Here is my answer.

It is a fallacy to assume that in the interest of preserving mankind's freedom of choice God limits what He is able or willing to do. This line of thinking is fallacious in more ways than one.

First, it is nowhere taught in the Bible. The terms "free will" and "freedom of choice" are not found in the Bible. You will find the terms "will" and "choose" in many places, but these terms are never discussed or used in connection with the term "freedom." And nowhere does the Bible indicate that God has placed limits of any kind on His power or ability to accomplish whatever He sets out to do. As a matter of fact, you will find many verses and passages that indicate exactly the opposite (see Isaiah 14:24, 27 and 46:9-10).

Part of the fallacy of assuming that God somehow limits Himself by giving mankind freedom of choice is the assumption that this is some kind of trade off that God makes. It is nowhere taught in the Bible that God allows bad things to happen, mainly sin and suffering, in order to preserve human freedom. The truth is that God created a flawed world on purpose and with loving intent. He gives us the freedom to fall into sin and experience both good and evil in our lives because this is necessary for our spiritual growth. It is impossible to develop good or positive traits in isolation from their evil and negative counterparts. God does not allow or permit things to happen which are not in accordance with his perfect will. When an omniscient and all-powerful God permits something to happen, it's because He wants it to happen.

Another fallacy related to the above is the false notion that God is unable to influence our behavior without restricting our freedom of choice. God can easily cause us to freely make the right choices, simply by shaping our thoughts and desires. This in no way violates our freedom to choose. He does this in a variety of ways that are amply illustrated in the Scriptures.
Here are some examples:

The Holy Spirit convicts (or convinces) us of our sinfulness (John 16:8). God works in our hearts to convince us that we are sinners in need of a Savior. Through the Holy Spirit He opens our spiritual eyes and enables us to see the truth, not only about our sin, but also about our need for God's remedy, Jesus Christ.

The converse is also true. When it suits His purpose God also can (temporarily) harden our hearts and blind us to the truth. There are numerous references to this in the Bible, the most famous of which is the hardening of Pharaoh's heart prior to leading the Israelites out of bondage in Egypt (Exodus 9:12).

Similarly, God in New Testament times hardened the hearts of His own chosen people in order that the Gospel might be more easily spread to the Gentiles. Please carefully read Romans 11:25-32. Here we learn that Israel's blindness was only temporary, until the *"fullness of the Gentiles has come in."* Afterwards, *"all Israel will be saved."*

Paul's conversion in Acts, Chapter 9, is an example of God's direct, dramatic, and miraculous intervention to convince Saul, a persecutor of Christians, that His views regarding Jesus were completely erroneous. Paul was one of those Israelites who were temporarily "blinded" to the truth. God used this occasion to open his eyes.

There would be no point to intercessory prayer if we did not believe that God is able to change people's hearts and draw them to Christ. It was Paul's heart's desire and prayer that Israel be saved (Romans 10:1). When God gave us freedom of choice, He did not totally relinquish control over our lives. God does not make our decisions for us, but He is fully capable of influencing our thoughts and attitudes of heart which comprise the motivation for the decisions that we make.

Evangelism and preaching of the word are another way that God influences our thoughts. In addition to correct attitudes of heart, information is also needed. We cannot possibly freely choose to receive Christ as our Savior and Lord if we have never heard of Him or if the information we have about Him is erroneous. So, a very important tool God uses to influence our decision to receive Christ is the sending out of messengers, armed with Gospel information. See Romans 10:14-15.

Rewards and punishments in this life and the next are another way God influences the moral and spiritual decisions that we make. In Matthew 6:19-21, God motivates us to live righteous lives in order to lay up for ourselves *"treasures in Heaven."* The converse to positive motivation is the negative kind, which takes the form of various punishments and chastisements in this life and also in the next.

Technically, free agency is not the same as free will. This I have made clear, but for God's purposes it accomplishes the same thing. Free agency allows us the perception and experience of having free will and allows us to make right and wrong decisions and bear the consequences of those decisions. As a result of these subjective experiences we learn first-hand about good and evil and experience spiritual growth. Free will is technically an illusion, but a very useful one from God's perspective.

A good analogy would be setting up a military training exercise in an artificial setting. For the participant, the experience seems very real and the result is pretty much the same, as if the learning took place under actual combat situations. God actually takes this a bit further and does not actually inform the participants that they are only experiencing a simulation which is taking place under very controlled circumstances. That makes the experience even more "real" for the participant. The nice thing about this training exercise that we call life is that God remains in control and does not permit matters to get out of hand, as might be the case if He granted us genuine free will and took away all the restraints, as in the case of an actual combat situation.

For our wills to be completely free God would have to completely restrain Himself from intervening into our lives to influence our decisions. The extent to which God intervenes and influences our decisions is the extent to which our freedom of will is restricted.

The conclusion of the matter is this. By allowing the freedom to choose, God in no way limits Himself. He is still fully capable of eventually bringing us all to repentance by influencing our wills by the various means noted above. This, I believe, defeats the argument that God's doing so would somehow violate man's supposed free will.

Universal Restoration

The obvious resolution to the Calvinism vs. Arminianism debate is the doctrine of Universal Restoration which in my view is plainly taught throughout the Scriptures. It doesn't really matter if our choices in life are "freely" made or not. God has already decided that eventually all will come to Christ, each in his own turn, some sooner, some later. All will receive the same reward in the end. Since God is the ultimate cause of all our decisions, it fitting that He gets ALL the credit.

Ephesians 2:8-9: *"For it is by grace you have been saved, through faith--and this is not from yourselves, it is the gift of God--not by works, so that no one can boast."*

I love the Parable of the Vineyard. It beautifully illustrates the above principle.

Matthew 20:1-16: *"For the kingdom of heaven is like a landowner who went out early in the morning to hire men to work in his vineyard. He agreed to pay them a denarius for the day and sent them into his vineyard. About the third hour he went out and saw others standing in the marketplace doing nothing. He told them, 'You also go and work in my vineyard, and I will pay you whatever is right.' So they went. He went out again about the sixth hour and the ninth hour and did the same thing. About the eleventh hour, he went out and found still others standing around. He asked them, 'Why have you been standing here all day long doing nothing?' 'Because no one has hired us,' they answered. He said to them,*

'You also go and work in my vineyard.' When evening came, the owner of the vineyard said to his foreman, 'Call the workers and pay them their wages, beginning with the last ones hired and going on to the first.' The workers who were hired about the eleventh hour came and each received a denarius. So when those came who were hired first, they expected to receive more. But each one of them also received a denarius. When they received it, they began to grumble against the landowner. 'These men who were hired last worked only one hour,' they said, 'and you have made them equal to us who have borne the burden of the work and the heat of the day.' But he answered one of them, 'Friend, I am not being unfair to you. Didn't you agree to work for a denarius? Take your pay and go. I want to give the man who was hired last the same as I gave you. Don't I have the right to do what I want with my own money? Or are you envious because I am generous?' So the last will be first, and the first will be last."

Chapter 12

The Nature of Reality

I would like to begin by summarizing what I believe is the fundamental nature of reality, based on modern physics.

According Einstein's general theory of relativity, E=MC², energy equals mass times the speed of light squared. When you reduce matter to its fundamental component, you end up with pure energy, which in a manner of speaking has no substance to it. Substance, or mass, may be converted into pure energy, and vice-versa. Just a tiny bit of mass may be converted into a huge amount of energy, which is what happens during an atomic explosion.

The same holds true at the sub-atomic quantum level. It has been demonstrated through actual, indisputable, verifiable, repeatable, and almost universally accepted scientific experimentation that the external physical world we observe is actually immaterial. The smallest individual particles, which make up all physical objects, continually blink into and out of existence. In the exact present moment in time, they exist only in the form of waves of potential energy, described by mathematical wave functions, which do not actually collapse into realities (ie. particles) until actually observed by conscious observers.

One experiment that demonstrates this truth is the famous double-slit experiment relating to Heisenberg's uncertainty principle which states that you cannot determine the future state of any particle based on its current position and velocity. When you "observe" or "measure" the position and/or velocity of a wave-like photon of energy, it "collapses" into a particle, and that particle can end up virtually anywhere. You cannot determine in advance where the particle will be the moment after you observe it. Most likely it will end up where you expect on the detector screen on the other side of the two slits, but in actuality it can end up anywhere in the universe based on a range of probabilities. It has been deduced by many physicists that the universe we observe does not actually exist. No two individuals or particles exist at the same moment in time in relation to one another. Everything is "relative" according to Einstein's theory of relativity. You are separated from everything you physically observe by the amount of time it takes the light to travel from the object you are observing to the retina of your eye. Even two related subatomic particles, such as protons and neutrons in a single atom, do not occupy the same place in time relative to one another.

It has been scientifically verified and universally agreed upon that the smallest possible unit of time is approximately 1×10^{-24} seconds (one Planck unit of time) and the smallest unit of distance is approximately 5.3192×10^{-44} meters (one Planck unit of distance). In between those units nothing exists. When a particle moves the distance of one Plank unit of space, it technically disappears and ceases to exist during transit and comes into existence again on the other side, with no time transpiring during transit. That is why the electrons of an atom move only in clearly defined orbits around the nucleus. When they move from one energy level (ie. orbit) to another, they disappear and cease to exist during transit, and then they instantaneously appear at the next energy level, without any time elapsing during transit. This is referred to as a quantum leap.

What we are viewing when we observe any object, whether in motion or not, are the discontinuous frames of space/time (similar to the frames of a movie) which occur at very small intervals measured in Planck units. In between those frames things only exist as waves of probability or possibility, which do not actually collapse into actual objects (ie. particles) until they are observed by a conscious observer. The actual "present" that I am observing consists of an empty vacuum of nothingness, only un-collapsed waves of potential energy, described by physicists as quantum wave functions. The energy waves that "collapse" into particles by

106

our observations exist in the present moment in what physicists call a "super positioned state" and exist only as possibilities with an infinite number of potential outcomes spread out over all of time and space. The actual "present" moment of the universe from my unique perspective in space and time may be best described as a quantum vacuum, containing nothing but potential energy.

Because of the time it takes for light to reach the retina of my eyes, everything I am looking at in this current moment is in the past. It does not actually currently exist. Everything in the future does not yet exist. So from my perspective, nothing actually exists except my own consciousness, which is not actually a part of this so-called physical universe. I am a spiritual, non-physical, being viewing the world through the eyes, ears and brain of a quasi-physical body.

These discoveries completely changed the way scientists understand the nature of the universe. The old system of Newtonian physics that described all events as deterministic in nature based on strict laws of gravity and motion had to be abandoned in favor of the indeterminism of quantum mechanics. On the macro level (large things), Newtonian physics pretty well describes how the physical universe works, and the results of our measurements are very predictable. But on the micro or quantum level (very small things) we are not able to make accurate predictions and are only able to describe future events as a range of probabilities, not certainties. When events at the quantum level combine to create large objects and events that we can see and experience with our physical senses, we end up with a world at the macro level that is totally unpredictable. True randomness actually does exist in our universe. We don't live in a natural world subject only to the natural laws of Newtonian physics. We actually live in a supernatural world that is partly described by quantum mechanics and general relativity. We are not physical beings subject to deterministic immutable laws of cause and effect. We are actually supernatural, spiritual beings. We live in a world that is governed only by probabilities and possibilities.

You might ask, if events don't actually happen until after I observe them what observer or observers are collapsing all the other wave functions of possibility that I don't observe? What about the tree in the forest that falls when no one is looking? Does it really fall? Perhaps it does, perhaps not. I will say this, human beings are not the only conscious entities in the universe. God is the "conscious observer" who views everything from every possible time and place. All "lesser" conscious entities, including the entire human race, are actually all part of a single divine Godhead. God observes and experiences the created universe, not just "through" us, but "as" us. God may be described as a universal collective consciousness. We are all individual aspects of the consciousness of God. God is everyone and everything that exists. He is omnipresent and omniscient. There is nowhere that God does not exist. It is impossible to be separated from an omnipresent God.

One way to illustrate this is to compare the collective consciousness of God with a colony of bees. The individual bees exist as separate conscious beings, but they are invisibly connected to one another, and collectively they operate as a single larger organism. Each separate organism operates with a degree of autonomy, but it is also a part of a larger organism, called a hive or colony, which has a personality of its own that incorporates and combines the personalities of the entire colony. In some ways, it behaves as a single conscious entity. At the same time, the individual bees, act as separate entities. In this illustration, we would be the individual bees, and God would be the hive.

Now I would like to answer a question that relates to the apparent randomness and uncertainty of the positions and velocities of the objects that collapse (ie. materialize) as a result of our individual and collective conscious observations. Are the resulting velocities and positions of the particles and objects purely random, or is there some form of guidance involved? Are all human events the result of blind chance, or are they somehow being guided by our individual thoughts and purposes in combination with those of the collective consciousness, which is God? In other words, in addition to causing the quantum waves to collapse into actual particles, are we in any way able to at the same time influence the future velocities and positions of those particles?

In my view, there are two irrefutable proofs that the results of quantum collapse are not totally random and that the universe that we experience and observe is not the result of blind chance. The first proof is the fact that the creation and continued existence of the universe requires a level of fine tuning that is mathematically impossible to achieve by merely random processes and must be the result of some kind of intelligent design. The second proof is the increasing order and complexity that we see in the development of life on Earth, which, according to the second law of thermodynamics, should not be happening. According to this law, which is accepted by the majority of the scientific community, random processes should inevitably result in disorder, but instead we see increasing order and complexity.

God, in a manner of speaking, may be described as a universal conscious entity who brought the universe into being and controls its evolution and development by means of nothing more than His thoughts and active observations. Because we are spiritual beings, and individual parts of the consciousness of God, it is very possible that we have the ability to creatively influence the outcomes of our individual lives by means of that same process, subject perhaps to certain limitations imposed for the good of the entire collective. There is truth to the Biblical teaching that with God *"all things are possible"* (Matthew 19:26) and that when we draw upon this limitless resource through prayer we are literally capable of *"doing all things"* (Philippians 4:13) and that *"nothing will be impossible"* for us (Matthew 17:20).

Because we are spiritual beings, created by and connected with God in the way described above, I believe our thoughts, including our attitudes and prayers, can have a dramatic effect not only on future outcomes in our own lives but also in the lives of others whose lives we touch. I believe that for this to happen, what we are praying for must not be at cross purposes with God's plans for all of us (ie. the colony). For example, if individuals are approaching an intersection from two different directions and both are "praying" for a green light, both prayers cannot be answered in the affirmative. God has an overriding blueprint which determines the general outline, purpose and culmination of all future events. He allows us great flexibility with respect to the individual routes we choose to travel, so long as the overall plan is not compromised (see 1 John 5:14-15). The result is an interesting and sometimes confusing interplay among God's sovereignty, quantum uncertainty, and mankind's freedom of choice.

The Virtual Reality that We Call Life

Assuming the above description of reality is true, what would be the meaning and purpose of it all? Why would we permit this world of our own creation to be filled with so much human misery and evil? The answer to these questions might surprise you. Here are a couple of illustrations that I think will help. They are based on the notion that the world we live in is not actually real, but is more like a computer simulation instead. Because it is not real, and only a simulation, we can't be hurt by it. However, we can still learn from it.

For example, airline pilots train in computerized flight simulators before being allowed to fly solo in an actual aircraft. The reason for this is obvious. If you crash the plane in a simulator, you walk out alive. Flight simulators create an artificial environment that seems so real that the trainee can for a time forget that the experience is not real. The same kind of learning takes place in a simulator as would occur in an actual airplane, but without the danger. There is one major problem with this type of training, however. Because the trainee knows he is only in a simulator, he might be tempted to bend the rules and/or engage in unsafe practices, knowing that if he makes a mistake he/she will still be able to exit the simulator unscathed. A better way to conduct the training exercise would be to erase the trainee's memory of his existence prior to entering the simulator and convince him that he is actually in a real airplane.

110

That is exactly why, when we are born into this "simulated" world, our memories have been erased and we don't remember our prior existence in heaven and don't remember who we really are. If one is going to use a simulated world for a training exercise, then it must seem real to the learner. I don't know about you, but this world seems pretty real to me, and the threat of death is also very real. Sin and evil in this world seem very real to me, as well, and their influence on my attitudes and behavior are also very real. This simulated reality that we live in works the same as an actual world because we think that it is real. The learning potential is only maximized, however, if the deception is convincing. Haven't you often wondered why God does not communicate with us in clear and unmistakable ways, and demonstrate to us beyond any reasonable doubt that He exists and that Heaven awaits all of us when we die? Well, now you know why. If He did this, He would destroy the illusion and diminish the effectiveness of the simulated training exercise that we call life.

I take comfort in knowing that God has placed me in an earthly environment that is only a simulation, and for that reason it is completely safe. My real home is in heaven, and during my training exercise here on earth, God is with me. He is always by my side. The worst thing that can happen to me is that I crash the plane (ie. die physically). At that point, I would wake up from the illusion, having exited the simulator, and prepare to try again.

Here's another illustration, one that might help you understand why God allows sin and evil to exist in this simulated world. Let's suppose you are a typical family and you are able to purchase a computerized virtual reality game. When your family programs the game's computer and puts on their virtual reality helmets they are all transported together into the game and find themselves immersed in a holographic world of sights and sounds that closely approximate an alternate reality. When the game is over, the lights go back on, and they all remove their helmets and resume their lives in the real world. Then they all get together and choose a new setting and story line for the next time they play. Lots of fun, and just a game.

Now, let's suppose you as parents would like to teach your children not to become bullies at school. So, you program your virtual reality game to simulate a school setting, and when you put the helmets on the heads of your children they find themselves in a virtual reality where they are nerds and misfits in a school full of bullies. Now, you know that your children are going to experience some scary moments and a great deal of unpleasantness, and they might not handle themselves very well in that situation. At times, they would forget they are in a game and would be genuinely afraid of those bullies. While they are in the game, they would not be in any real danger, because it is only a simulation and they are actually seated right in your living room with their virtual reality helmets on. But they wouldn't know that. For them it is not a game but an actual reality. After the game is over, and they have been awakened from their virtual reality dream, you sit down together with them and talk about what happened and what they learned. This bears a striking resemblance to the life review, which is part of most Near Death Experiences (NDE's). Can you see the wisdom of this kind of learning? Now that your children know what it's like to be on the receiving end of bullying, they are much less likely to become bullies at their real school.

To carry the analogy one step further, suppose the family played the simulation game more than once, each time changing the cast of characters they would meet and interact with in the game, in order to learn new lessons and further develop their character. One time, they might decide to reverse roles and the children become the parents, and the parents would become the children, and so on. At the conclusion of each game, they would meet together, carefully analyze and evaluate what happened, and discuss what they learned from the experience. For each new game, they would change the rules of engagement and tailor the situation and cast of characters to help them achieve specific developmental goals.

112

Well, I personally believe that is exactly what happens in real life. I have done an extensive amount of reading on the subjects of Near Death Experiences (NDE's) and reincarnation, and I am convinced beyond any doubt that they are real and genuine. The evidence is very strong. It is not within the scope of this book to make the case for reincarnation. I will only say here that it fits very nicely with the latest findings of quantum physics and general relativity, and also with extensive research that has been performed and well-documented regarding the existence of life after death, and the existence of the human soul independently from the physical body. Most people who refuse to believe in NDE's, out-of-body experiences, past life and between-lives hypnotic regression, children's memories of past lives, communications from the dead through mediums and clairvoyants, and the like, have not read very extensively on those subjects. Most skeptics dismiss these concepts for one of three reasons. They have been told by their religious leaders that these ideas are in conflict with the teachings of the Bible, or they are hard-core atheists and skeptics, or they simply have not done their homework and carefully and thoroughly read up on the subject.

Because I come from an evangelical Christian background, I will say this. If you are a Christian fundamentalist and believe that the Bible is infallible and inerrant, including all of the Old Testament, then some of these teachings will definitely conflict with the Bible as you have been taught to understand it. If, however, you view the Scriptures as I do, not as the actual word, or words of God, but instead as a human, yet still inspired, record of mankind's changing, evolving and improving views about the nature and character of God, culminating in the teachings of Jesus and His apostles, especially the Apostle Paul, then you will find much support in the Scriptures for what I have explained above.

When properly translated, interpreted and understood, I believe the Bible totally supports the universality of God's love for all mankind, His intention to redeem all humanity from sin and death, the existence of the spirit or soul independent from the physical body, life after death for everyone, the fair and equitable judgment that we all face after death for things we have done in the flesh, God's willingness to forgive even His enemies, salvation from sin and the fleshly sin nature by grace (which is undeserved love), the rule of love, rather than assent to a narrowly defined set of religious dogma, as the main criteria for God's evaluation of our thoughts and deeds while on earth, Jesus' oneness with the Father, our oneness with Jesus Christ and the father, Christ living in us and we living in Him, our current existence in heaven (ie. seated with Christ in the heavenly places), the Spirit of God dwelling in us and empowering us to live Godly lives and perform miracles of love and healing, and much, much more.

All of this ties in perfectly with reincarnation. The goal of our earthly walk is to become like Christ. For most of us, this is an ages-long process. It is accomplished not in our own strength, but by the power of the Spirit of God within us, which is, in a manner of speaking, our own human spirit or soul, our divine nature, which is directly connected with the God of ALL creation. Everything I have read in the literature describing life after death, reincarnation, and the nature of God supports the view that the single word that most accurately describes the nature of God is Love. Love is literally what makes not only this world go around, but all other worlds as well, including all of the unseen heavenly places.

Chapter 13

Materialism, Dualism, and Idealism

The three "isms" given above represent three world views that are common to scientists, theologians, and just plain ordinary people like you and I. These world views directly influence the way we process information. Our world view influences many of the underlying assumptions, or premises, that we begin with when we perform certain types of theological or scientific investigations. If the underlying premises are false, then even a flawlessly conducted investigation will yield a flawed result.

I believe that faulty underlying premises are the root cause of many paradoxes or contradictions that scientists and theologians are forced to live with after their investigations have been concluded. That is why equally brilliant individuals can arrive at totally different conclusions after examining exactly the same information. For example, if an evolutionary biologist has a materialist philosophy and begins his investigations with the assumption, or premise, that God does not exist, he would most certainly conclude that the evolutionary process is guided by random chance and nothing else. He would have to live with unexplained gaps in the fossil record, and results which are in conflict with the universally accepted second law of thermodynamics. If a Biblical literalist examines the same evidence, he might conclude that the geological strata were laid down by a single cataclysmic event, the Genesis flood, just a few thousand years ago. He would have to live with apparent contradictory evidence that these strata were laid down over millions of years. Or he might conclude that the universe and the earth were created with the illusion of age built in.

During the course of my scientific and theological research and inquiry I have come to appreciate the brilliance and impeccable logic of those who disagree with me. Nevertheless, it would be pointless to engage in debate with them, because the underlying premises which form the basis of their logic are not the same as mine.

This brings me to a discussion of the three "isms" mentioned in the title of this essay. These three different world views form the basis of our logic when we read the Bible and formulate doctrine. The materialists believe that everything is material in nature. To them, even our thoughts are nothing more than electrical and chemical processes which occur in our physical brains. If you begin with this premise when examining the Bible, your conclusions are going to be quite different from those of a theist and/or dualist. A dualist is a person who believes that the material and the supernatural worlds are separate and distinct. Most Christians are dualists. They believe that because God is separate from the physical world, He needs to intervene "supernaturally" to influence the course of human events.

The idealist, on the other hand, has a totally different world view than either the materialist or the dualist. The idealist believes that the physical and the spiritual worlds are one and the same, and there is no difference between the natural and the supernatural. The idealist believes that both the spiritual and material dimensions of reality are comprised of and created by the "thoughts" of God and to a lesser extent those of other conscious beings created by God. Some quantum physicists also view reality in this way. They believe that the present universe that we observe currently exists only in the form of un-collapsed quantum waves. These waves do not actually collapse into reality until observed by God and/or other conscious observers. This has been demonstrated by repeatable and universally accepted experimental data. To date, no viable alternative has been offered. Not all physicists are idealists. As a matter of fact, the overwhelming majority are died-in-the wool materialists, despite the experimental evidence to the contrary. As a result, materialist physicists are forced to live with

116

many as yet unresolved contradictions and paradoxes associated with quantum physics.

In like manner, religious dualists must live with many unresolved contradictions and paradoxes associated with their belief systems. Most Christians, and also many non-Christians, are dualists. They view almost all theological issues in black and white terms and approach all religious inquiry with an either/or mentality. This forms the basis of their world view and is one of the underlying premises on which their logic is based. Here are some examples of these "black and white" dualisms: God vs. Satan; good vs. evil; physical vs spiritual; Heaven vs. Hell; saved vs. lost; God of love vs. God of wrath; faith vs. logic; grace vs works; the Bible is literally true or not true at all; and so on.

When studying the Bible and searching for spiritual truth, our logic is flawed if we begin with the premise that there can only be two possible results for each inquiry. If neither result is the correct one, then at the conclusion of our investigation we will inevitably be left with unanswered paradoxes and contradictions. The actual "truth" of the matter might lie somewhere in between two extremes, or it might be a solution that incorporates them both, or it might be something altogether different that disproves both of the alternatives you originally had in mind.

Dualism lies at the heart of religious fundamentalism. The opposite of fundamentalism, however, is not liberalism. Most liberals also think in dualistic terms, though perhaps somewhat less so than fundamentalists. Christian fundamentalists and liberals have more in common with one another than they do with the materialists.

Idealists, on the other hand, believe that the so-called material world is not actually material at all and is not really separate and distinct from God Himself and the spiritual world. According to them, everything created by God is a part of God. Many adherents of Eastern religions also view the world in this way. Idealism is far less common in Western thought.

If everything that exists is technically a part of God, created by God, and controlled by the thoughts of God, and if God is by nature loving and good, then everything that happens or exists must be consistent with God's character and would have a loving purpose. In other words, things or events that we would normally think of as at "cross purposes" with God's intentions (Satan, evil, suffering, hell, and the like) must instead fit into God purposes and be consistent with His loving nature.

As you approach the study of the Bible, don't be afraid to think outside of the box, so to speak. Do not dismiss out of hand all approaches to truth that might conflict with the prevailing dualistic Christian world view.

Studying the Bible with an open mind is a very scary proposition, especially for the Christian fundamentalist, because for this person a lot is at stake. Entertaining the possibility that he or she might be wrong about one of these very rigid fundamentalist doctrines could be viewed as an admission of doubt. Faith, in the view of many fundamentalists, is an absolute requirement for salvation. Without it, there is no chance of escaping endless, infinite punishment in Hell. Any open minded investigation which has the potential of eroding a person's faith is very scary. They are stuck in the black and white box of dualism. For them, God is either your best friend or your worst enemy. There is no in between. To them, God is extremely "schizophrenic," so to speak. He is an "either-or" God. Either He forgives and overlooks your sins or He never forgives you at all, and instead punishes you forever in Hell. You are either saved or you are not saved. Most fundamentalists will tell you they believe in God's unconditional love for all mankind. At the same time, their description of God's actual behavior is not even remotely consistent with that kind of love.

So, here's the problem. Because dualists begin their study of the Scriptures with the underlying assumption (premise) that people are either saved or not saved and are going to Heaven or Hell when they die, they interpret all the Scriptures they read in such a way as to be consistent with this dualism. As a result they have to live with huge unresolved paradoxes and contradictions, and a very schizophrenic God.

A few years ago, I embarked on a very scary journey of discovery. I decided to engage in a serious attempt to study the Bible with an open mind and see if it was possible to interpret the Scriptures in such a way as to retain the essence and truth of the Gospel, and at the same time remove the paradoxes and contradictions. I hope you can appreciate how scary this was for me. In order to be intellectually honest, I also had to entertain the possibility that the materialists might be right and the Bible is not true at all. My main criteria for interpreting the Scriptures was to accept the most natural interpretation and avoid as much as possible work-a-rounds and the twisting of meanings and semantic tricks in order to arrive at conclusions which were consistent with the result I was seeking. If the materialists were right, and the Bible was just a hopelessly flawed human document, then so be it.

The result of my investigation over a period of several years was a validation of most of the core beliefs of Christianity, but with some important differences. Most of the dualisms have been replaced by their idealistic counterparts. The one major doctrine that emerged, and made possible a resolution of the dualisms, paradoxes and contradictions, was the doctrine of salvation as a process, rather than an instantaneous event. Rather than viewing Christian salvation as an all-or-nothing condition, I now view it as a journey, a journey that we all share together. God loves us all equally and has only the best intentions for all of us. Each of us is at a different stage in that journey, and, in the end, none are left behind.

Chapter 14

NDE's, Reincarnation, and Christian Theology

I debated with myself and my family about whether or not to include this chapter in my book. Especially in evangelical Christian circles, this topic is very controversial, and believers in NDE's and reincarnation are regarded by many as unbalanced and victims of demonic deception. I decided to include the chapter, anyway, because, in my view, the scientific, and testimonial case for the validity of these experiences is very strong. At the same time, I don't believe there is any conflict between these teachings and the Gospel of Christ as I have presented it in this book. I believe it will be helpful for you to be exposed to this material, regardless of whether or not you believe it. Belief in these concepts has actually served to strengthen, and not diminish, my faith in Christ.

It is beyond the scope of this book to provide evidence for the validity of near death experiences (NDE's) and past-life and between-lives hypnotic regressions. Many books have been written about the subject, which I would encourage you to read for yourself. Literally millions of people have reported NDE experiences, and tens of thousands have experienced past-life hypnotic regressions in a clinical setting. If you are not comfortable reading about this topic, you may just skip this chapter of my book. Nothing in this chapter conflicts with any of the theological views expressed in the rest of this book. What we learn from NDE's and past-life regressions is in complete harmony with the Scriptures as I understand them. I believe that NDE's and past-life regressions are the most reliable forms of communications from Heaven and the afterlife, mainly because they are "eye witness accounts." Other forms of communication from the "other side" mostly take the form of second-hand accounts that are "channeled" by a third party such as a medium or clairvoyant. In my view, the second and third-hand accounts are less reliable because they are more subject to fraud and deception.

I am sure we are all puzzled by the differences in the NDE experience from one individual to the next. There are also many similarities. I believe the experience is real, and not based on thoughts that occur in the physical brain, because most of the subjects are "brain dead" during the NDE experience. I do believe that our human consciousness exists separately from our physical brain, and all sensory experiences of our lives are stored not only in the brain but in our spiritual consciousness as well. I believe that what is going on during the NDE is a kind of shaping of our own individual realities. Apparently, in the Heavenly realms we are to a great degree able to create our own realities. This also occurs during our earthly plane of existence, but to a much lesser degree. Quantum theory ties in very nicely with this. *"As a man thinks, so is he."* After death, some people can remain trapped for a while by their negative thoughts which are holdovers from their earthly existence, while others are liberated. So in the NDE's we do see a variety of both Heavenly and sometimes "hellish" experiences and settings. Those experiences, though varied, are still real. After death, each of us experiences a different reality because we come from different places in our thinking and all have different issues to work out.

What we see in the NDE experience is a picture of what happens immediately after death. We don't ever see is what comes later, because people who experience NDE's always return to their physical bodies. For information about what happens afterwards we must rely on past-life and between-lives hypnotic regressions. Psychiatrists discovered the art of past-life regression quite by accident. While regressing their patients backwards in time during hypnosis to discover childhood events that might be impacting a patient's current well-being, occasionally one of those patients would accidentally regress to a previous life. Sometimes an individual would regress to a place between lives in Heaven or the

121

spirit world. Over the years, many therapists have made past-life regression their main practice. Some therapists have regressed literally thousands of patients to their past-life and between-lives states. Often these sessions are tape recorded and mediculously documented. Information coming from these sessions has been verified over and over again as accurate and which could not be known by the subjects from any other information sources. For example, sometimes the subjects speak in languages they knew from a previous live but cannot speak in their present life. Sometimes they exhibit a knowledge of historical and cultural details about times and places that they have never been exposed to in their current life.

It is interesting to me that what happens between lives in Heaven is remarkably consistent from one patient to another, much more so than with the NDE experience. Amazingly, thousands of patients from all backgrounds and religions, even atheists, report pretty much the same things. Apparently, once we get past the initial stages of entering the Heavenly realms and make a cleaner separation from our life on earth we all tend to end up in similar circumstances.

Based on most near death experiences (NDE's), it appears that God's judgments in the afterlife, or Heaven, initially take the form of a life review. During the life review we observe every detail of the life we have just lived from our own perspective and also from the perspective of those whose lives we have touched. We are able to see and feel how our actions are affected others. We feel their joy if we did something good to them, and we also feel their pain and anger if we caused them physical or emotional harm. Here's where the cross of Calvary comes in. Almost all NDE accounts of the life review describe the experience as totally non-judgmental in nature. And almost all report an overwhelming experience of unconditional love and acceptance by God. During the life review the individual feels as though he or she is judging or evaluating him or herself. God is not the judge. Instead, God is the one who is viewed as dispensing unconditional love. The message of Calvary is that Christ made atonement for everyone's sins. Most who encounter God in the NDE experience are pleasantly surprised at God's non-judgmental attitude towards them and how much God loves them, despite their sins and shortcomings.

I do not believe that we enter the Heavenly realms with fully reformed characters. I believe that more learning and character development will take place after we die, either in the Heavenly realms or in future incarnations on Earth. In between our earthly incarnations much learning takes place, including the life review and a needs assessment. In addition, some very interesting group learning sessions take place as well as very high tech forms of "book learning." Lots of time is also allotted for various forms of recreation and enjoyment. After much time goes by, we then decide with the help of our friends and guides in Heaven when and where to reincarnate. The particular time, place and body that we choose for our next life on earth depends on what lessons we want to learn. Spiritual growth occurs much more rapidly during an earthly incarnation than in Heaven for obvious reasons. In heaven there are no pain, sorrow, or problems of any sort. Learning and growth takes place much more rapidly in the difficult and challenging environment here on Earth where we are exposed to real life and death situations. It is on earth where the "rubber meets the road," so to speak. The lessons we learn in the "crucible" of our earthly life can be viewed as a purification, refinement, and self-improvement process. No one achieves perfection in one lifetime. As I have said many times in this book, I believe that growing into the likeness of Christ is an "ages-long" process.

Much of the eschatology (doctrine of the last things) of the Bible suggests that rewards and punishments will occur during physical ages to come on planet Earth. Some, called Preterists, believe that the Kingdom Age actually began two thousand years ago, and that Christ is growing and perfecting His Kingdom right now on Earth. I personally am sympathetic with the Preterist view. I also believe that the descriptions of God's Kingdom ages in the Book of Revelation are mostly symbolic and allegorical in nature. Reincarnationists would say that rewards and chastisements of God are carried out during our current and future lives here on Earth and between lives in Heaven.

Some of you might be wondering, when do we meet Jesus in Heaven? This is a difficult question for me to answer because most people who experience NDE's make no mention of Jesus. Some Christians identify a "being of light" as Jesus, while some non-Christians identify this being as a religious figure from their own religious tradition. Most don't recognize this being by name or as any particular religious figure. After progressing further into the heavenly realms, this "being of light" is often recognized as a "spirit guide" who was assigned as one's teacher during the time spent in between lives. A spirit guide, and other entities as well, act as "guardian angels" during our incarnations here on earth.

The name Jesus was given to Christ during his earthly existence, but He would not necessarily be called by that name in the afterlife. The "Jesus of history" and the "Christ of faith" are indeed one and the same, but the name Jesus belongs for the most part to the earthly life of the Christ, who in a larger sense is the divine *"Logos,"* the co-creator of the universe. When the Bible speaks about every knee bowing at the *"name"* of Jesus, those worshippers were not technically bowing to a name, but instead to the person who bore that name during His earthly sojourn. It is not the name Jesus that we worship. Instead, we worship Christ Himself.

The descriptions of God the Father in most NDE's and between-lives regressions are very impersonal. God is mostly referred to as the "source," or "creator," or the "energy" from which everything is made and holds together. The Creator is always described as incredibly loving. Love is the chief attribute by which God is described. God is further described as the greater whole of which we are all a part. There is a strong sense of connectedness in Heaven. We are all connected with God and with each other. I believe that Christ is the only begotten Son of God, the first-born of all creation, and the entity through whom everything else was created. But in Heaven this "person" of the Godhead is not called

124

Jesus. I would guess that most of what Christ does in Heaven is done behind the scenes, similar to the way He works on Earth. There are many levels of exaltation or *"dwelling places"* in Heaven. Not all of these levels are accessible to most of us. It takes untold ages to progress to the highest levels where Christ may perhaps be known in a different way. In the meantime, we all remain indwelt by the Spirit of Christ by whom we are all connected with each other. In Heaven, as on Earth, we would still be regarded as Christ's body, His hands and feet as it were, through whom He accomplishes His master plan of transforming all of His created beings into His own likeness. Of course, Christ is not really a "he" or a "she." In Heaven, these anthropomorphisms no longer apply.

Chapter 15

Situational Ethics
and the Law of Love

Situational ethics has long been maligned by religious conservatives, for obvious reasons. It is troubling that in our modern society we are experiencing a breakdown in traditional morality, with the devastating consequence of the breakdown of the family. During the turbulent social upheaval that occurred in the 1960's, one of the catch phrases was "if it feels good, do it." During the period of the Judges in Israel, the nation ignored the commands of God and the people *"did what was right in their own eyes."* When we lose our connection with God, there is a strong tendency to lose our moral compass and engage in all sorts of sinful and destructive behavior.

In Jesus' day, the religious authorities went too far in the opposite direction and established a very complex and detailed moral code of behavior. Often, the letter of the law violated the spirit and intent of the original precepts on which it was based. There were so many do's and don'ts that the people lost touch with the reasons why those laws were created in the first place. In the Sermon on the Mount, Jesus addressed this problem by redefining several of those commands in such a way as to conform to their spirit and intent. Jesus crossed many social, religious and ethical boundaries, in both word and deed, when He reinterpreted the commands of Scripture to conform to the one law that supersedes and overrides them all, the law of love. Every law that God has given to us is based on His love for us, and He wants us to be like Him. Jesus summed up the Law with the two commands, that we love God with all our heart and our neighbor as ourselves. According to 1 John 4:7 *"Beloved, let us love one another, for love is from God, and whoever loves has been born of God and knows God."* Christ has set us free from the demands of the Law, according to the Apostle Paul. Because our standing with God is based on grace, not works, Paul said, *"I have the right to do anything. . .but not everything is constructive."*

The law of love does not give us license to do as we please or make up our own rules, regardless their negative impact on others. It does however, give us the option of departing from some of the commands of Scripture that were culturally based and no longer apply today. Here are examples I chose for purposes of illustration.

The Case for Abstinence from Alcohol

In 1 Corinthians 10:23-33, the Apostle Paul makes a compelling case for abstinence. In verse 23, he points out that though many activities may be permissible, not all are necessary or constructive. Paul made the personal choice to avoid eating meat sacrificed to idols, even though there was nothing inherently wrong with this practice. But for the sake of the *"weaker brethren,"* who believed this practice to be wrong, Paul abstained from eating this meat. Paul did not want by his example to influence others to engage in a practice which they thought sinful, thereby wounding their consciences and *"causing them to stumble."*

Although there is not a direct correlation between drinking alcoholic beverages and eating meat sacrificed to idols, Paul teaches us a principle here which does apply. It is perfectly OK for me to drink alcohol in moderation, so long as I can control my behavior and not drink to excess. But I need to understand that by doing so I may cause a Christian brother to stumble, if because of my example he begins to drink in moderation and eventually becomes an alcoholic. It might be that he is genetically or psychologically predisposed to alcoholism, or he may not have the same ability as I to cope with the stresses of life that can in some cases lead to alcoholism. This principle especially applies to us as parents. Our children are very strongly influenced by our behavior. If we drink alcohol our children are likely to do so as well. The same holds true for other potentially addictive behaviors, such as smoking, gambling, and drugs, none of which are expressly forbidden in the scriptures. Total abstinence, therefore, represents the first line of defense in overcoming harmful addictions in the individual lives of Christians and in the lives of those for whom they become centers of influence, such as family members, friends and acquaintances, and church brethren.

Divorce, Slavery and Homosexuality

The ancient Hebrew society was highly patriarchal in nature. Women were regarded mostly as possessions and not as equal partners with men. They were treated like property, with ownership transferring from the Father to the husband. They could even be sold as slaves. Men could have as many wives and concubines as they wanted. Men could divorce their wives, but wives could not divorce their husbands. Women were punished for adultery, but not men. Women were not allowed to participate in many important religious ceremonies. In some places in the Old Testament, women were treated similarly to the way they are treated by ISIS and the Taliban. They were not allowed to leave the homes of their fathers or husbands. They were restricted to economic roles with little or no authority. They could not testify in court. They were not permitted to talk to strangers. They were required to wear head coverings and veils in public. The list goes on and on. Jesus did not directly address most of those issues, but he did address the issue of divorce. He emphasized the sanctity of marriage and limited the justification for divorce to adultery. At the same time, he also taught that women should not be permitted to remarry, regardless of the reason for the divorce.

I have often wondered why Jesus didn't go further and condemn all restrictions against women. The Apostle Paul also accommodated the customs of his day regarding women's rights. He believed that women should remain subservient to their husbands, remain silent in church, cover their heads, and not wear braids. Over time, cultural mores change, but ever so gradually. Paul never spoke out against slavery, even though one of his friends and church members was a slave owner. Both Jesus and the Apostle Paul, I believe, were products of their culture, but even in areas where they might have disagreed with the popular culture, they were careful to pick the right battles. I believe the same was true with regard to other cultural issues such as slavery, homosexuality, eating meat that had been sacrificed to idols, and so on.

Most important to Jesus and the Apostle Paul were the internals, not the externals. They gave us guidelines to follow when deciding which aspects of the Hebrew laws to obey. They were mostly concerned with the spirit and intent of the law, rather than the letter. Jesus said that all the law can be summed up in only two commands, that we love God and love our neighbors as ourselves. The Apostle Paul said this: *"All things are lawful for me, but all things are not expedient. All things are lawful for me, but all things do not edify."*

For me, this does not give us license for immorality, but it does give us license to depart from some of the cultural norms of the ancient Hebrews, in cases where there is no violation of the rule of love and where our actions will not be a stumbling block to the weaker brethren. Society has evolved tremendously for the better over the past two thousand years, at least in most parts of the world. During the past couple hundred years or so in this county, we have made tremendous strides with the issues of women's equality, slavery, and human rights. Sadly, this has been accompanied by a relaxing and erosion of morals and certain beneficial codes of conduct. I believe that as Christians, we do need to be sticking out like sore thumbs and adhere to a much higher standard of morality than what we find in the general culture. At the same time, however, I do believe that we need to make a distinction between the letter of the law vs. the spirit and intent of the law and not be afraid to depart from cultural practices which violate the law of love that Jesus taught.

I won't be trying to tell you what position you should be taking on the issues of marriage and divorce, premarital sex, abortion rights, homosexuality, and the like. I would just encourage you to examine those issues in light of the principles given above and try to be as gracious as possible with those who disagree with you.

Chapter 16

The King and the Crown Prince

I would like to conclude with a story that will add some flesh to the theological bones contained in this book.

The king's reign was nearing an end. During his reign, poverty and corruption were rampant throughout the kingdom, making life miserable for all but the ruling elite and their favored minions. Both the rich and the poor were equally corrupt. The rich cared only about themselves and exploited the poor, and the poor not only hated the rich but they also did not care very much for one another, and they fought bitterly over the meager rations that were left to them.

The king was fully aware of the current state of the kingdom. In the past, it was thought by all that a truly egalitarian society could be achieved by means of strict legislation and a system of enforcement from the top down. Rulers were put in place and given the task of enforcing the rules and maintaining order. The system the king had put in place did not work because the rulers abused their power and completely disregarded the king's mandates. Instead of using their power and influence for the good of the people who were placed in their charge, they exploited them and treated them harshly and cruelly.

They ignored the king's edicts and believed they could do whatever they wanted with impunity, for two very good reasons. First, they had the king outnumbered, they believed. If they stuck together, it would always be the many against the one, and they would always have the upper hand. Secondly, they were confident that even if the king had the power to stop them, he would not do so. Experience had taught them that the king rarely intervened to correct their behavior. They logically assumed that the free-hand that had been granted them by the king would continue indefinitely.

Actually, the king was much wiser than they realized. The current miserable state of affairs was part of a great and noble plan. The people were kept in ignorance of this plan for two very good reasons. First, the plan would not work if the people were aware of it. Secondly, the next part of the plan would not be possible without the failures associated with the first part. Failure is an important part of any learning process.

With the end of his reign in sight, the king was finally ready to turn over his kingdom to the crown prince, the sole heir to the throne. It would be the task of the crown prince to restore order to the kingdom by completely doing away with the present kingdom and creating an entirely new one in a completely different location. The transition from the old to the new kingdom would not be sudden. Time would be required to prepare everyone for life in the newly rebuilt kingdom.

The crown prince would begin the process by going undercover and mingling with the populace, disguised as one of them. There are two reasons for this. First, he wanted to demonstrate under real-life circumstances exactly the type of attitudes and behaviors that would be required for life in the new kingdom. Secondly, he wanted everyone to know exactly how much he loved and cared for them. He began by carefully selecting a few initiates, all of whom were from the lower classes, who would become the initiators of the great transition from one kingdom to another. He strictly admonished them not to tell anyone who he was, not until the time was right. He provided them with many proofs of who he really was, and very patiently and painstakingly taught and demonstrated to them the attitudes and lifestyle that would be required for entrance into the new kingdom.

In the new kingdom, the rules of law and the enforcement penalties would be replaced by a completely different system. The new system would be based on only one rule, the rule of love. There would be no need for the enforcement of this rule, because a strong desire for obedience to this rule would be built into all of the subjects. In other words, it would be impossible for anyone to break the rule, because it would be against their very nature. In the beginning, the initiates had great difficulty understanding and accepting this. Their biggest question was this. How is it possible that anyone could achieve this level of perfection? How is it possible that anyone could qualify for entrance into this new kingdom? The crown prince, without telling them exactly how the process would work, just told them to trust him and that all things are possible.

After a few years, when he felt the initiates were ready to carry on without him, the crown prince initiated the most important part of his plan. He would demonstrate his love for them in a way they would never forget. He wanted them to fully understand and believe the power of love is more than able to overcome and completely do away with the powers of hatred, greed and selfishness. He voluntary allowed himself to be tortured, humiliated and killed as an ultimate demonstration of not only his self-sacrificing love for them, but also of his commitment to non-violence. In the future kingdom, the rule of love will not be enforced by force or violence, but instead by the power of example. At any time during this process the crown prince could have revealed his identity and invoked the power of the king to set himself free. But, this would have completely nullified the lesson that he was teaching.

Another very important lesson the crown prince taught them came after he died. He rose up from the grave and proved to them that there is life after death. It turns out that in order to gain entrance into the new kingdom one first must pass through the veil of death.

After this, the crown prince returned to his father and together they implemented the next phase of the transition from the present kingdom to the next. Together, they would watch over each of their subjects individually. No longer would their care be entrusted to surrogates who might abuse their powers. They would personally accompany and guide each individual as they gradually transform themselves and ready themselves for life in the new kingdom. Because each individual is in a different stage of progress, provision must be made for stops, or dwelling places, along the way. As each person crosses the veil of death and arrives on the other side, they will be met by other guides and helpers and helped along their way. Because no one arrives on the other side with a fully-reformed character, they are directed to temporary dwelling places where they will continue to grow and develop. In the new kingdom, there will be many different dwelling places, each one perfectly suited for the level of advancement achieved by the dwellers.

Many who cross over will not be ready for life in the perfected new kingdom. They, instead, will be forcibly detained in dwelling places separate from the others, until they can be trusted to voluntarily abide by the rule of love. The important thing to keep in mind is that no one is abandoned forever by the king in these places. They are continually being watched over by the king and his son, and many guides and helpers are sent by the king to these places to act as angels of mercy to teach them and ultimately rescue them and help them transition to better environments.

So where is all this headed? The entire transition process takes place over many ages, or eons of time, until every single one of the king's subjects has entered the kingdom, fully perfected.

Appendix

Leftovers from Richard's Kitchen
Additional Thoughts & Reflections

What Is Forgiveness, Really?

Forgiveness is not the same as exoneration.
It does not remove the guilt of the offending party.

Forgiveness is not the same as reconciliation.
It does not necessarily restore relationship with the offending party.

Forgiveness is not the same as forgetting.
It does not remove the memory of the offense.

Forgiveness is not the same as pardon.
It does not remove the need for correction.

Forgiveness is not the same as responding to a request.
It does not require a confession and request for forgiveness.

Forgiveness is not something that a person receives from another.
It is instead something that a person gives to another.

Forgiveness is not something that a person deserves.
It is instead something that is given freely and unconditionally.

Forgiveness has not taken place if feelings of animosity persist.
It is instead a process of replacing animosity with compassion.

134

Forgiveness has not taken place if self-righteousness persists.
It is instead regarding oneself as intrinsically no better or worse than the offender.

Forgiveness has not taken place if one feels victimized by the offender.
It is instead realizing that all things work together for the good of those who express love.

Forgiveness is not about the forgiven.
It is all about the forgiver.

To err is human.
To forgive, divine.

Entering the Kingdom and the Law of Sowing and Reaping

The Jews of Jesus' day, even Jesus' closest followers, viewed the Kingdom as a physical kingdom that would be inaugurated with the coming of the Messiah. The message of John the Baptist, and of Jesus, was *"repent for the Kingdom of Heaven is at hand."* Later in His ministry, Jesus revealed that God's kingdom was not a physical kingdom, but a spiritual one, and that it was already in our midst (see Luke 17:21).

Interestingly, according to Jesus, entrance into the Kingdom had little to do with theology and more do with how you treat people, especially the poor. Jesus believed that even his adversaries, the chief priests and the elders, would be entering the Kingdom, but there would be tax collectors and prostitutes entering ahead of them. In the words of Jesus to those rulers, *"Truly I tell you, the tax collectors and the prostitutes are entering the kingdom of God ahead of you."*

Entering the Kingdom is something we will all be experiencing sooner or later. The term does not refer to literally entering into a physical kingdom on earth, or even in Heaven for that matter. It is a metaphor for entering into relationship with God and receiving rewards in Heaven, after death, for the good that we do in the flesh. Most of Jesus' stories and parables had to do with the accumulation of rewards in Heaven, and those rewards were based on how we treat the poor and those in need. The story of the Rich Man and Lazarus was not about theology. It was about how in the next life the tables are turned, with the poor being comforted and the callous rich being punished for their lack of concern for the poor. In the story of the separation of the sheep and goats, the Lord did not ask who prayed the sinner's prayer, but instead He asked how they treated the sick, poor and downtrodden. I believe that many so called "Bible-believing" Christians will be among those who are turned away for a season of *"age-during chastisement"* (literal translation). The judgments of God are based on how you treat people, not on how correct or incorrect your profession of faith (ie. your theology) might be.

Professing faith in Christ does not exempt you from the law of sowing and reaping. Rewards in Heaven are not based on what we believed about God while on earth, but instead on the love and compassion that we demonstrated towards those in need. We were all saved by grace on the Cross of Calvary, but the working out of our salvation, and the shaping of our characters into the likeness of Christ, is an ages-long process.

Trust me, we'll all believe in God after we die. Sooner or later, God will clue us all in on the correct theology. By then, however, it will be too late to back up the clock and live our lives again according to Godly principles. *"...it is appointed for man to die once, and after that comes judgment."* (Heb. 9:27) If you have been wondering what God's will is for your life and what God would have you do to serve Him, take a look around you and see what you can do for those who are less fortunate than you. Jesus said that when you do it to them, you are doing it to Him, even if you are not aware of it at the time, even if you are not yet a Christian.

What Happens when We
Turn to a Different Gospel?

"I am astonished that you are so quickly deserting the one who called you to live in the grace of Christ and are turning to a different gospel which is really no gospel at all." (Galatians 1:6-7a)

In Galatians, Paul made the case that when you rely on your good works for salvation, you are turning to a different Gospel, the result of which is condemnation. Paul is not saying that when you do this you will be eternally condemned to Hell. What he is saying is that you are wrong. That is all. You are guilty of *"foolishness"* (see Galatians 3:1). You do not forfeit your salvation. You merely lose the benefit of it.

He used Peter and Barnabas as examples of how foolish it is to hold onto the old idea that works of the Law are necessary for salvation.

"When Cephas came to Antioch, I opposed him to his face, because he stood condemned. For before certain men came from James, he used to eat with the Gentiles. But when they arrived, he began to draw back and separate himself from the Gentiles because he was afraid of those who belonged to the circumcision group. The other Jews joined him in his hypocrisy, so that by their hypocrisy even Barnabas was led astray." (Galatians 2:11-13)

Note the use of the word "condemned." Peter and Barnabas were condemned, but they obviously did not lose their salvation. They only lost the benefit of it, which is the joy of knowing that we are loved and accepted by God just as we are and that we are saved by grace, not works.

Please believe me when I tell you that no one ever went to Hell for trying too hard. When you turn to the false Gospel of salvation by works, all you are doing is making it harder on yourself than necessary. When you fall from grace, God does not love you any less.

Does this mean that good works are not important? Of course not, but the true Gospel of Christ, the Good News that we are saved by grace, does change our motive for doing good. We do it because God has made us good by nature. We do not serve God out of fear and under threat of punishment, but instead out of love and gratitude.

Inch by Inch, Anything's a Cinch.

According to the Chinese proverb, "a journey of a thousand miles begins with a single step." Another proverb goes like this, "inch by inch, anything's a cinch." Christian salvation, I believe, is an ages-long process that begins by entering into a relationship with Christ and does not end until the conclusion of the ages. In the words of the Apostle Paul in Philippians 3:13-14, *"I do not consider myself yet to have taken hold of it. But one thing I do: forgetting what is behind and straining toward what is ahead, I press on toward the goal to win the prize for which God has called me heavenward in Christ Jesus."*

When we enter into relationship with Christ we become *new creatures.* (2 Cor. 5:17) Old things pass away and all things become new. This is not an instantaneous process. It is a life-long journey that I believe continues after death. Progress, not perfection, is the best indicator that we have been genuinely "converted" to Christ. We all struggle with sinful habits in our lives, and like all addictions, they are very hard to break. Some are impossible to overcome without God's help.

Here's a suggestion for those of you who are struggling with a major problem or goal in your life. Try and break down the solution into very small bite-sized pieces, or steps. Decide what your first step will be, and make a commitment to do it each day, religiously, no matter what. Continue to do this until it becomes a daily habit and becomes a part of your lifestyle. Daily habits can be difficult to form, often with many missteps along the way, but once formed, they are just as difficult to break. Once you have formed your little "first-step" habit, then take another very small step, and form another habit that will advance your progress towards overcoming a major sin problem or achieving any positive life goal.

You Can Catch More Flies with Honey than with Vinegar.

Have you noticed that the largest, and fastest growing, churches in our country today almost never mention Hell in their worship, or in their sermons, or in their Bible studies? Nearly 100% of the focus in these churches is on principles of Christian living and on how much God loves us in Jesus Christ. Why is that? If the main purpose of the Gospel of Christ is to rescue people from everlasting torment in Hell, why is this aspect of the Gospel message almost never spoken of? Well, I can tell you why. If those dynamic preachers were to give everlasting Hell a place of prominence in their sermons and Bible studies, their churches would quickly be emptied.

A frequently expressed criticism of Christian Universalism is that it would remove the incentive for missions and outreach. I believe that the contrary is true. Many Universalists have the same passion for missions and outreach as believers in ECT (Eternal Conscious Torment), actually more so in my case, because I know that the Gospel of Christ is good news for all. The main religion of Japan, Shintoism, is based on a worship of, and reverence for, one's ancestors. Missionaries to Japan, in the early days, were forced, due to their incorrect theology, to proclaim, along with the message of salvation in Christ, that there was no hope for their ancestors, who they believed were eternally lost in Hell. Is it any wonder that Japan, despite our best efforts, remains largely unreached by Christianity?

Separating the Sheep from the Goats

When the nations were gathered before Christ in Matt. 25, and the sheep were separated from the goats, Jesus didn't ask, "OK, which of you prayed the sinner's prayer before you died?" When the teacher of the law asked Jesus what he must do to inherit eternal (aionian) life (Luke 10), Jesus didn't answer, "simply pray the sinner's prayer." The religion of Jesus is a "way" of life, not a "get-out-of-jail-free card." That is why the early Christians were called "followers of the way." All have been "saved by grace." That happened at Calvary. Now Christ asks us to live accordingly.

Wisdom Should Not be Equated with Certitude.

"The whole problem with the world is that fools and fanatics are always so certain of themselves and wiser people so full of doubts." Bertrand Russell

When I was young I felt cursed by my intellect, because I was unable to "prove" to myself the truth of Christianity. Though I desperately wanted to be "saved," I never felt that I qualified, because I was told over and over again that in order to be saved, one had to "believe." How on earth was one to know what "level" of belief was required, since belief can only be measured in degrees, and is rarely "absolute?" The more I tried to believe the more inadequate I felt. The more I tried to understand Christian theology, the more new questions that arose in my mind. After a lifetime of searching (about 50 years since my spiritually troubled

140

youth), I do believe I have found most of the important answers. However, I still have many more questions than answers. Could it be that honest atheists might be "closer" to God than many Christians who refuse to think for themselves?

The Best Reward for Doing Good

"So when you give to the needy, do not announce it with trumpets, as the hypocrites do in the synagogues and on the streets, to be honored by others. Truly I tell you, they have received their reward in full." Matt. 6:2

The best reward for doing good is becoming a better person. We can "see" God and future rewards only by faith, not by sight. By definition, an "act of faith" is done in the presence of doubt. Otherwise we would not call it "faith," but "certainty." Of the three examples below, who do you feel is making the most progress towards the goal of becoming like Christ?

1. The church member who tithes to the church, knowing that God will *"open up the windows of heaven"* (as in Malachi) and bless him financially in greater measure than what was given.

2. The seeker who gives his life to Christ in order to escape the torments of Hell and go to Heaven after death.

3. The agnostic or atheist who joins the Peace Corps because he/she genuinely wants to help people.

I do believe that one of the reasons that God "hides Himself" from us, and does not provide us with absolute "certainty" on all doctrinal matters, is so that we might more easily become good simply for goodness sake. He wants us to be good, not for immediate or future rewards, but because we have actually become good people.

I know this is controversial, but I believe that even Christ had to live with a degree of uncertainty while on Earth, hence the agonizing outpouring of grief in His prayer at Gethsemane.

Is God the Author of Sin and Evil?

We are all prone to sin and helpless to avoid it. That's the way we're made. We are born with basically selfish desires. Babies are very self-centered and selfish by nature. They need to be taught to be unselfish and put the needs of others before their own. Evolutionists would say that our innate selfishness is a "survival" mechanism. So, in that sense you could say there is an obvious need for God to make us that way. Unfortunately, this basic "survival" mechanism also leads to sin, when we "harm" others for our own benefit. Obviously, God wants us all to rise above our basic "carnal" desires and learn to love people unselfishly. So, while our natural built-in selfishness serves a good purpose, from a "survival" of the species standpoint, God created us for more than just survival. This built-in selfishness also serves the higher purpose of creating the circumstances that result in our need for His love and forgiveness.

There would be no merit in doing good if we were not also capable of doing evil. One benefit of this is that in our fallenness, we most appreciate God's love and mercy. To fully appreciate God's love and forgiveness, we must first find ourselves in need of it. I just don't see where God's perfect nature is diminished in any way when He creates us with a built-in need for His love and forgiveness. As a matter of fact, I think it's an act of pure genius on His part. We cannot find true happiness and fulfillment except in union with our Savior God. God created us with a "built-in" need for a loving relationship with Him.

What about Hitler?

Believe it or not, God loves Hitler just as much as He does anyone else. Have you ever heard the phrase, *"There, but for the grace of God, go I?"* If you had the same genetics and life experiences as Hitler, you might well have made many of same bad decisions as he. Christ died for all, and He saves all. The worse our "sin" condition, the more glory we give to God for our salvation. Most people resist the doctrine of universal reconciliation because they believe that people like Hitler "deserve" to go to Hell for all eternity. Conversely, they must also believe that they, on the other hand, "deserve" to go to heaven. Well, you can't have it both ways. If we are saved by grace, apart from works, so must Hitler become saved in the same manner. Christ made atonement for the sins of everyone on Calvary, including Hitler. It might take a bit longer for Hitler to "work out his salvation," but God will get the job done. It is God who saves us, and not we ourselves. God has all "eternity" (age upon age) to get the job done. One day, at the end of the ages, death will finally be abolished, and Christ will have drawn every last individual to Himself, as He promised He would, and we will all be presented *"faultless before the throne of God,"* and God will be *"all in all."* See Ephesians 2:8,9, John 12:32, Philippians 2:10-11, Ephesians 1:9-10, and especially 1 Corinthians 15:22-28.

The Key to Successful Christian Living

We need to know that God loves us and accepts us as we are. We all have "sins" that we are not yet willing to let go of. Destructive behaviors are like "addictions" and are extremely difficult to overcome. And it seems that no matter how hard we try to be better, there is always more that we could do. We deal not only with "sins" of "commission" but also with sins of "omission." I had the hardest time earlier in my life learning to believe that God wanted to bless me despite my unwillingness and/or inability to live up to what I have now come to realize are impossible standards. I do believe the Apostle Paul was onto something as he repeatedly emphasized the fact that our standing with God is based on grace rather than good works. Technically, in the words of Paul, *"all things are lawful."* God doesn't hold our sins against us. Successful Christian living flows from our relationship with God. It's not the other way around. Although I hate much of Augustine's theology, he hit the nail on the head when someone asked him how to make correct moral decisions. He answered, *"Love God and do as you please."* First God loves us and saves us. Then He helps us deal with our sin. It's not the other way around. He loves to give good gifts to His children. When we look up at Him and pour out our soul to Him and ask for His blessings and help, it melts His heart. Yes, God has emotions. He will always give us, in those moments, exactly what we need.

Why Atheists Hate Christianity

The fundamentalist view of a vengeful and cruel deity provides rich fodder for militant atheists. I once heard a panelist on the TV show hosted by Madeline Murray O'Hair, say this: *"The Christian God hides from view and makes it very difficult for people to believe in Him, and then condemns to everlasting torture in Hell all those who don't."* That statement really shook me up and bothered me for the rest of my life, until I finally changed my theology and my view of God. If Christians are ever to fully evangelize the world, they are going to have to start preaching the "good news" of the true Gospel, that God is the Father of all and loves us all unconditionally. Can you imagine how differently non-Christians and atheists would view Christianity if we were to do this?

My View of Bible Inspiration

I don't believe God is good because the Bible says God is good. I believe the Bible because it says God is good.

The Moral Dilemma of Compartmentalization

We are not normally disturbed by the misfortunes of others unless we actually make physical contact with them. While leaving choir rehearsal one night, I walked past a man who was sitting in the doorway of the church in much distress. He was a mess and would not make eye contact with anyone as we walked past him on our way out. A minute or two after I drove away, my conscience got the best of me and I circled back and eventually found him outside on the other side of the church crying uncontrollably. He said his wife just kicked him out for the last time and he had walked about 15 miles from there to where he now was. He was filthy and unkempt and apparently all of his worldly possessions fit in a very small knapsack. Both he and his wife, who were on public assistance, were addicted to drugs, fought all the time, and he was prone to violence. To make matters worse, she has a small child. I couldn't persuade him to let me take him back home or anywhere for help. Eventually he walked away and didn't want me to follow. I did anyway, gave him some money, and left him there in the freezing cold. I felt so helpless.

Of course, I was emotionally devastated by this. At the same time, I was reminded that the world is full of such people, and almost 100% of the time, I do not actually care at all, and feel no strong emotions about the plight of the homeless, as I did this evening. It reminds me of the Gaither chorus, singing and praising the Lord, with huge smiles on their faces, and at the same time believing that most of the rest of the world is going to suffer eternal torment in Hell. We do tend to compartmentalize our lives and our feelings, and tend to concern ourselves only with those people with whom we come into close physical proximity.

I'm not saying this is right or wrong. It only illustrates why people are able to believe in eternal torment in Hell for most of humanity, without being bothered by it.

Just so you know, the way I decided to handle my moral dilemma with respect to what happened last night was to become a regular contributor to the Jesus Center, in a town nearby, whose mission it is to minister to people like the one I was personally unable to help that night.

God's Self-Adjusting Universe

In a manner of speaking, does not evil punish itself? Has God not set moral laws in motion, by which we sow what we reap? Could it be that the chastisement and correction by God might happen not directly by his hand, but would instead result from the laws He has set in motion? Conversely, would not goodness and love create their own rewards in our hearts? God has created a universe which is to a great extent self-adjusting.

Little Things Can Make a Big Difference

I once had an acquaintance in college who was different in one small respect from anyone else I knew back then or have ever known since. You might ask, what was so very special about this person? Well, he wasn't particularly religious, and he posted playboy pictures on the wall of his dorm room, which I thought was quite immoral. Here's why I never forgot him. Every once in a while he would do something nice for one of us, without being asked. He would make someone's bed, or clean up someone's space in their dorm room, or present one of us with a small, thoughtful gift. I almost never think about anyone else I knew during my four years of living in that college dormitory, but I have never forgotten him.

Hudson Taylor, a great man of God and founder of the China Inland Mission, once said, *"A little thing is a little thing, but faithfulness in little things is a great thing."* In the words of Rick

Warren, *"small tasks often show a big heart."* Jesus said, in Luke 16:10, that *"whoever can be trusted with very little can also be trusted with very much."*

When you find yourself heartsick, depressed or discouraged, take time to do a small favor for someone else who could use a lift. See if it doesn't lift and enlarge your own heart as well.

The Goal of Christian Missions

Matthew 28:19,20 – *"Therefore go and make disciples of all nations, baptizing them in the name of the Father and of the Son and of the Holy Spirit, and teaching them to obey everything I have commanded you."*

Romans 10:15b – *"How beautiful are the feet of those who bring good news!"*

Which makes the most sense to you?

Plan A: The goal of Christian missions is to save people from the wrath of an angry God and help them avoid everlasting torture in a place called Hell. The message goes something like this. *"Hi folks, I would like to introduce you to the Gospel of Jesus Christ. If I can persuade you to sincerely pray this simple, one or two sentence prayer, you will go to Heaven when you die. If you don't, then when you die you will be tortured for all eternity in Hell, along with all the rest of your ancestors and loved ones, who weren't lucky enough to hear and respond to this wonderful good news of the Gospel."*

Plan B: The goal of Christian missions is to make disciples of all nations, introduce them to the Savior of the world, Jesus Christ, and teach them to obey His commandments. The message goes something like this: *"Hi folks. God loves you and so do I. God demonstrated His love for you by dying on the Cross of Calvary in* *the person of His Son, Jesus. The penalty for sin is death, and it was paid in full for all of you on that cross. The price only had to be paid once, so all of you are off the hook. God offers to each of you the opportunity of experiencing a personal relationship with Him and His Son, Jesus Christ. When you enter into relationship with God, He will give you many wonderful gifts including, but not limited to, love, joy, peace, patience, kindness, goodness, faithfulness, gentleness and self-control in this life and also in the next life after you die."*

Happiness Comes from Within

The happiest people I ever knew were the people I met in the early 70's while stationed in Thailand during the Vietnam War. Most of the Thai people were dirt poor and lived in small, cramped apartments in a hot, humid climate with no air conditioning. When you walked down the damp, dingy streets, you were greeted with huge smiles everywhere you went. The rice paddies and tropical fauna held no attraction at all for me, but the Thai people thought they lived in the most beautiful place on Earth.

I, myself, could hardly wait to get out of Thailand and get back to the 'States. During my 2-year stay, I continually daydreamed about living back in the 'States again, especially in some beautiful, forested area with a temperate climate and many rivers and lakes. To me, Thailand was an ugly, dirty place, and I had a difficult time understanding why the Thai people were so happy all the time.

After returning to the 'States, I quickly moved to a place near the rivers and lakes and forests similar to what I had envisioned while in Thailand. For a while, life was great. Eventually, after settling into marriage and a career, life got a little bumpier and I found myself overwhelmed much of the time by financial pressures, and the various trials and tribulations that we all face in life, no matter where we live. During the times of greatest stress, I wished that I had opted for a simpler, less expensive lifestyle. I often thought of those happy Thai people in Thailand who were poor in material goods, but rich in so many other ways.

Just as beauty is in the eye of the beholder, so it is with happiness. It may be found in almost any circumstance. If the external circumstances of your life are making you unhappy, look within for the help you need.

"Do not be anxious about anything, but in every situation, by prayer and petition, with thanksgiving, present your requests to God. And the peace of God, which transcends all understanding, will guard your hearts and your minds in Christ Jesus." Philippians 4:6-7

Sin Is Our Enemy, Not God

It has been asserted by many evangelical Christians that no one is "good enough" to be saved. Some would go so far as to insist that even if a person were guilty of only one sin, and perfect in every other respect, God would be just in condemning that person to everlasting torment in Hell. The idea is that God demands perfection from us.

The actual truth of the matter is just the opposite. God is love. He is more loving and forgiving than any human being. Because of this, there is absolutely no need to qualify for salvation. We are not saved by works, because works are not necessary. They are not necessary because God loves us just as we are. We are slaves of sin, true. But sin is our enemy, not God. Jesus did not come to save us from God. He came to save us from sin, from our own self-destructive behaviors. God is the *"Savior of all men, especially those that believe"* (1 Timothy 4:10). God is the one who saves, not the one who condemns. According to John 3:17, *"God did not send his Son into the world to condemn the world, but to save the world through him."*

"For by grace you have been saved through faith. And this is not your own doing; it is the gift of God, not a result of works, so that no one may boast." Ephesians 2:8-9

La La Land or Law Law Land

It seems that most people are uncomfortable with shades of gray, especially with respect to Christian theology. Most of us like to wrap up our religious, moral and ethical concepts into neat little "dualistic" packages. We view people as either saved or lost, basically good or basically bad, saved by grace or saved by works, spiritual or carnal, and going to only one of two places when we die, Heaven or Hell.

Some of us live in spiritual La La Land, and view Christian salvation as something that is a gift of God, given by grace, with no judgment of their sins after that. They view their conversion experience as obtaining a ticket into Heaven where they will not be held accountable for their sins.

Others live in spiritual Law Law Land, and view Christian salvation in the same dualistic terms, but instead of being saved by grace apart from works, they view it as something that one achieves by obeying God's laws. Hopefully, on judgment day after they die, the scales of God's justice will weigh in their favor.

Whether in politics, religion or everyday life, the truth of the matter generally lies somewhere in the middle. We are saved by grace, apart from obedience to the Law, but we are still held accountable by God for every sinful thought or action, even every careless spoken or unspoken word. Being saved by grace, does not exempt us from the "Law of Sowing and Reaping." God doesn't stop loving us when we fall into sin. However, because He loves us He allows us to suffer the negative consequences of our sinful actions in order that we might grow and learn from those experiences. What loving and caring human father would not do the same for his children?

"...the Lord disciplines the one he loves, and he chastens everyone he accepts as his son." Hebrews 12:6

How to Get the Dirty Bone
Out of Your Dog's Mouth

"Do not get drunk on wine, which leads to debauchery. Instead, be filled with the Spirit." Ephesians 5:18

We all have sin addictions, some great and some small. This is part of being human. We always fall short of God's best for us. The best way to overcome sinful habits and addictions is to focus on the positive, not the negative. If you want your dog to let go of that dirty old bone he just dug up in the back yard, you won't succeed by trying to yank it from him. If, instead, you offer him a nice juicy steak, he will drop the old bone in a heartbeat.

If you can get in the habit of rededicating your life to God's service anew each morning in prayer, and remain in a "state of prayer" throughout the day, just one day at a time, you will find yourself replacing bad attitudes and habits with good ones. Start out each day with a fresh infilling of the Holy Spirit, and as the day progresses "top it off" over and over again as the level drops. Don't worry about the specifics of how to overcome an addiction or bad habit. Don't worry about how to rid yourself of bad thoughts. Just focus on filling yourself to overflowing each day with the love of God. Understand that God loves you just as much when you fail as He does when you succeed.

It's not easy to curse your neighbor and praise God at the same time. They are mutually exclusive activities. I can assure you that the latter activity is much more pleasurable than the former. Love is so much more gratifying than hate. Freedom is so much more pleasurable than addiction. God is much better company than fair weather friends who tempt you to sin. Keeping busy with the Lord's business is so much more gratifying than sitting around doing God knows what else and hoping for nothing bad to happen because of it.

Finally, don't worry about results. Results will come eventually, sometimes all at once, sometimes a little at a time. Your God is a God of miracles, so don't worry about the "mechanics" or the "how-to's" either. Look within for the help you need. Yes, God is out there, but He is also in you and will give you whatever strength you need to overcome any negative habit.

Believers Will Enter the Kingdom ahead of Unbelievers

"Jesus said to them, "Truly I tell you, the tax collectors and the prostitutes are entering the kingdom of God ahead of you. For John came to you to show you the way of righteousness, and you did not believe him, but the tax collectors and the prostitutes did. And even after you saw this, you did not repent and believe him." Matthew 21:31-32

Since becoming a Christian universalist, I notice little things in the Scriptures that support universalism, things that I never noticed before. In the above passage, which I read in church today, Jesus pointed out that the tax collectors and prostitutes would enter the Kingdom ahead of the chief priests and elders of Israel. The reason is that the tax collectors and prostitutes believed the Gospel message and the chief priests and elders of Israel did not. Notice that Jesus did not say unbelievers would never enter the kingdom, only that believers would enter first. Interesting, huh?

The Pearl of Great Price

"Again, the kingdom of heaven is like a merchant looking for fine pearls. When he found one of great price, he went away and sold everything he had and bought it." Matthew 13:45-46

The wonderful gift of *"aionian"* or *"age-abiding"* life (usually mistranslated as *"eternal"*) escapes many so-called "born-again" Christians. When we view our reward as something external to us, something that we receive after death in a faraway place called Heaven, we miss out on the joys of Heaven within that are available to us right now.

An interesting analogy would be Jesus' parable about the *"pearl of great price."* When we read this parable, many of us might view it as some sort of treasure hunt. Somewhere, in the depths of the ocean, lies an oyster, with a beautiful pearl inside. In order to find it, we would need to rent a boat, perhaps hire a guide, and diligently scour the ocean bottom in search of it. The search for this pearl could be very long and arduous, and very few would be able to find it.

My theological studies over the past few years have led me to the understanding that each of us has a hidden identity as a child of God. In the deepest recesses of our consciousness, we are all intimately connected with God. The oyster that contains the pearl of great value is not to be found somewhere at the bottom of the ocean. Instead, we are the oyster, and the pearl actually lies within us. To find it, we need to look within.

Christian salvation is not an instantaneous event, based solely on a one-time confession of faith whereby we ask an external God to come to us and dwell within us. In my view, salvation should be visualized as a process of discovering our true identity as children of God, already redeemed by Christ. It is the process of discovering and experiencing the Kingdom of God (ie. the rule of Christ) that already exists within us. God loves us unconditionally before we become saved in our conscious awareness. It is not God who changes when we experience salvation. Instead, it is we who change. We don't have to be anxious about whether or not we qualify by our faith or works for salvation. We don't have to worry about the timing of it, or how long it might last. All of us are loved and accepted by God, just as we are, right now. All that remains for us to do is recognize it and experience it.

The God Within

Philippians 4:13   *"I can do all things through Christ who strengthens me."*

When I was a young man, I would look up into the sky at night and contemplate the immensity of the universe. This made me feel very small and insignificant, and I would wonder how or why a God, who is even bigger than the universe, would take time to focus on me. How could God be in a million places at once and pay attention to millions, perhaps billions, of simultaneous prayers all over the planet? For this reason my prayers lacked power and effectiveness.

Over the past few years, my view of God has significantly changed. I now believe, based on my study of the Scriptures, quantum mechanics, and NDE's, combined with common sense and logic, that God is not some immense being who lives outside of the universe and merely looks in on it from time to time, taking time out of His busy schedule to listen to millions of prayers. I now realize that the universe and everything in it is actually a part of God. It is an extension of God's consciousness. In the deepest recesses of our consciousness we are not only intimately connected with God, we are actually made up of God parts, ie. spirit, and are part of God himself. We are actually God's "body." Paul refers to us as the "body of Christ," which to me is the same as saying the "body of God the Father," because Christ is in God the Father and God the Father is in Christ, and we are in Christ and Christ is in us.

154

In His prayer in John 17:20-22, Jesus prayed that we would all experience that oneness: *"I do not ask on behalf of these alone, but for those also who believe in Me through their word; that they may all be one; even as You, Father, are in Me and I in You, that they also may be in Us, so that the world may believe that You sent Me. "The glory which You have given Me I have given to them, that they may be one, just as We are one;..."*

I believe that deep within we are literally "one with God." Christian salvation is the means by which we become aware of this and experience it in our daily walk. We are the body of Christ through whom God experiences His creation. When we pray to God the Father, we are not just talking to a spiritual entity who exists separately from us. Yes, God is "out there." He is everywhere. However, He is also within us. He is us. To some this might seem blasphemous, but it is Scriptural. When we talk to ourselves, we are talking to God. He not only hears us, He is us. The Apostle Paul believed that he could *"do all things."* We don't have to depend on God to do everything for us. He has given us the power and authority to do things for ourselves. We have at our disposal the power of God Himself, within us, to accomplish almost anything we set our mind to. The only limitation is our lack of faith.

Understanding this has greatly helped me with my prayer life. I talk to myself a lot more than I did before. I pray now with more conviction. I know that if I am paying attention, so is the God the Father.

The Parable of the Persistent Widow

Luke 18:1-8 *"Then Jesus told his disciples a parable to show them that they should always pray and not give up. He said: "In a certain town there was a judge who neither feared God nor cared what people thought. And there was a widow in that town who kept* *coming to him with the plea, 'Grant me justice against my adversary.'*

"For some time he refused. But finally he said to himself, 'Even though I don't fear God or care what people think, yet because this widow keeps bothering me, I will see that she gets justice, so that she won't eventually come and attack me!'"

And the Lord said, "Listen to what the unjust judge says. And will not God bring about justice for his chosen ones, who cry out to him day and night? Will he keep putting them off? I tell you, he will see that they get justice, and quickly. However, when the Son of Man comes, will he find faith on the earth?"

God is not a reluctant judge who needs to be pestered continually before He answers our prayers. The point Jesus was making is that even an imperfect earthly judge will reward your persistence and eventually give in. God is more loving and just than any earthly judge and is more than willing to answer our prayers, especially when we persist.

There are two reasons why persistence is needed.

First, we need to wait on God's timing. God knows our situation better than we do. He knows when the time will be exactly right.

Secondly, when we pray we are drawing upon the power that God has already granted us within our human spirit to accomplish miracles. God works through us, not for us. He builds us up and empowers us to accomplish seemingly impossible tasks on our own. As Paul said in Phil. 4:13, *"I can do all things through Christ who strengthens me."* The more we visualize and focus on our goals and desires, the more concrete they become in our consciousness, and the more likely they are to manifest in the physical world in which we live. Practice makes perfect. The more we pray, the more powerful our prayers become. When we see positive results, we are encouraged to pray even more, and our faith grows stronger.

156

Ninety percent of what my wife, Arlene, and I pray for each morning is exactly, word for word, the same as the day before. I can tell you from personal experience that God answers prayer.

Like Father Like Son

Children tend to turn our like their parents. Often the child, even after insisting he or she will never be like a disliked parent. actually becomes like the parent anyway. Children of abusers tend become abusers themselves. Children who grow up in loving homes tend to do better in life than those who do not. The same is true when we regard our Creator God as a Heavenly Father. Christians are taught to emulate and try to be like the God they worship. This is a good thing, if God is pictured as loving, kind, fair, just and forgiving. But if God is at pictured as judgmental, harsh, hateful and cruel towards those who do not conform to a certain carefully defined set of attitudes and behaviors, then we give ourselves license to behave in exactly the same way.

When we teach our children that God is loving by nature, yet hateful and cruel towards His enemies, then we give them an excuse to be hateful and cruel towards their perceived enemies. The reasoning goes like this. It's ok to be judgmental and hateful towards those who deserve it. To make matters even worse, not only is it ok to be judgmental and hateful, towards those who behave badly, but also towards those who might be loving, kind and generous, but who's religious beliefs differ from ours, or who are different from us with respect to ethnicity, gender orientation, political views, dress standards, and so on. It's OK to hate people whom we feel God would hate.

While it is true that Jesus taught us to love our enemies and return good for evil, we don't take this teaching as seriously as we should. Why? Because we believe God does not take it seriously. If it's OK for God to be judgmental, hateful and cruel towards all non-Christians, especially towards egregious sinners, then why would it be so bad for us to behave in the same way?

We look for ways to circumvent God's command to love our enemies and return good for evil. For example, we might say God forgives His enemies, but only if they repent and ask for forgiveness. We even excuse hateful attitudes towards kind and loving people who don't repent of their incorrect theology, sexual orientation, or moral values. When we view God as both loving and hateful at the same time and highly selective regarding those whom He blesses and those whom He doesn't, then we can justify almost any negative attitude towards people who differ from us.

The schizophrenic God described above is not actually the real God of the Bible. I personally believe that most of the harsh and cruel acts of God described in the Bible, especially in the Old Testament, are not accurate history and mostly reflect man's imperfect view of God. However, even if you accept those accounts as true and accurate descriptions of God's activities, the Bible also teaches that after judgment, God shows mercy, and the purpose of God's negative judgments is to teach us life lessons and help us to learn and grow. The Bible clearly teaches in both the Old and New Testaments that God's plan for the ages is to restore all humanity to a state of perfection, bliss and union with Himself in Heaven.

The Four Spiritual Laws

Many of you have heard of the Four Spiritual Laws of Bill Bright and Campus Crusade for Christ:

1. God loves you and offers a wonderful plan for your life (John 3:16; 10:10).

2. Man is sinful and separated from God. Therefore, he cannot know and experience God's love and plan for his life (Rom. 3:23; 6:23).

3. Jesus Christ is God's only provision for man's sin. Through him you can know and experience God's love and plan for your life (Rom. 5:8; 1 Cor. 15:3 - 6; John 14:6).

4. We must individually receive Jesus Christ as Savior and Lord; then we can know and experience God's love and plan for our lives (John 1:12; 3:1 - 8; Eph. 2:8 - 9; Rev. 3:20).

Here, I humbly submit my own alternate version:

1. God loves you and everything that happens is part of God's plan for your life. According to Prov. 16:9, *"The heart of man plans his way, but the Lord establishes his steps."* Even our bad choices are part of God's plan.

2. Man thinks he is separated from God. Therefore, he doesn't always know and experience God's love and plan for his life. According to Romans 6:23, *"the wages of sin is death, but the gift of God is age-abiding life."* This verse has nothing to do with life after the death of the physical body. It refers to our awareness of and relationship with the God within all of us, our true spiritual selves. To be alive spiritually is to be connected with God in our conscious awareness.

3. Jesus Christ, God incarnate, showed us how we can know and experience God's love and plan for our lives. He demonstrated to us that although God's plan for us includes suffering and physical death, God never leaves us nor forsakes us. In order for us to be born again spiritually, we must first experience death. According to John 12:24, *"unless a kernel of wheat falls to the ground and dies, it*

159

remains only a single seed. But if it dies, it produces many seeds."

4. If we obey Christ and follow his teachings and example, we can experience spiritual life in the here and now, not just after we die physically. According to 1 John 5:12, *"Whoever believes in the Son has eternal life, but whoever rejects the Son will not see life, for God's wrath remains on them."* Just as separation from God is an illusion, so it is with God's wrath. The experience of rejection by God, or spiritual death, may be replaced with the abundant life for those who believe in Christ and follow his teachings.

Taking Hold of God

If God seems aloof and unreal to you, and if your prayers seem to go unanswered, may I offer you this advice? You are a spark of the divine, a child of God, created from God's own spiritual DNA. If you are listening to your own prayers, God is listening. As long as I believed that God was "out there" somewhere, bigger than the universe, I felt very isolated and alone. When I began to realize that the Spirit of God permeates every cell in my body and that I am one of the many "faces" of God, through whom He experiences His creation, I was able to appreciate how close and intimate my relationship with God actually is.

You and fallible, vulnerable, people like yourself are the means by which God intervenes in people's lives. God expresses Himself through the many of His own personalities that He has placed on this earth. If you want to find God and experience His presence in your life, look within, and also enter into loving relationships with others like yourself. Tell them they are not alone, that you love them and care for them. Jesus said that the greatest commandment is to love "God" and your "neighbor" as "yourself." Seek out people in need, people like yourself. Don't look for a sign from Heaven that God is real. Become the sign, and do your best to demonstrate the love of God to the people in your life, especially those who are closest to you.

The reason we can't find God or see God is that He is spirit and is undetectable to our physical senses. To experience God directly is a physical impossibility. That is why Christ came, so that we could catch a glimpse of who God is and what He is like. Jesus is the physical image of an otherwise invisible and unknowable God. Jesus is gone now, and has imparted to us His spirit and given us the task of expressing the love of God here on earth.

If you have trouble "holding on" to your faith, try "holding onto" the people you care the most about. When we hold onto one another we are taking hold of God and God takes hold of us. If your spirit has been crushed and you are barely hanging on, it's OK to turn to others for the help you need. When you lean on others for the help you need, you are leaning on God. Allow God to speak to you through the people in your life. Don't try to go it alone.

He Was There All the Time.

When we pray to God, or when we just talk to ourselves, we are communicating with God the Father. God hears even the smallest prayer. He is that close to us. God dwells in the hearts of his children. By the way, as in the Lord's Prayer, our Father also dwells in heaven. The interesting thing is that so do we. We are spiritual beings viewing the physical world through the eyes of our physical bodies. In reality, our true inner selves, which Paul refers to as the *"mind"* (as opposed to our fleshly body), we are spiritual beings (See Rom. 7). Yes, God resides in Heaven and so do we. In God we *"live and move and have our being."* Those words were spoken to the Pagan Athenians by the Apostle Paul. We are all God's offspring, intimately and forever connected with our Heavenly Father. As sinners in our fleshly bodies, we have lost our way and lost touch with this reality. We are all like sheep who have gone astray. Jesus promised that after He rose from the dead He would draw us all back to Him. The truth is that we have been in His presence all along, but just didn't know it. So, as a practical matter, we might as well have not been in His presence. Christian salvation is a process of reconnecting with God who was there all the time. I love the Christian gospel song, *"He was there all the time."*

A Broken Body Can Only Be Healed by Reattaching the Severed Members.

Have you ever thought about the separation of the *"wheat from the chaff"* not as a process of forever separating those who are saved from those who are lost, but instead as a refining process of removing the impurities from our individual selves and our "collective selves," as well? We are all connected spiritually because we all have within us seeds of the divine and we are all spiritually connected with one another as God's offspring (ie. children). Most of the "salvation" references in the Hebrew Bible (ie. the Old Testament) refer to a "corporate process" of refining a nation. References in the Hebrew Bible of judgment by fire most often refer to cleansing of the nation resulting in the salvation of the entire nation, and all the other nations of the earth, as well (See Zephaniah 3:8,9). Individual salvation did not take the form of going to heaven after death, but of one's name living on and being remembered by one's progeny. Individually, we all experience a "refining process," as well, both in this life and the next (See 1 Cor. 3:15) whereby the impurities are removed from our lives. Collectively, as with the Children of Israel, we are undergoing a corporate refining process, whereby the collective is purified by removing the dross. The difference is this. Because this collective "dross" consists of people, not just things or bad attitudes and behaviors, they cannot be "destroyed" (literally: lost) forever, but only until cleansed and purified and made fit for being grafted back in again to the collective (See Romans 11:24). Just as it is impossible for energy to cease to exist (it can only change forms),

162

so it is with the human soul or spirit. It cannot cease to exist. How can any part of God cease to exist or be lost forever? The collective is not healed by cutting off its members. The opposite is true. It can only be healed by reattaching its members and making the body "whole" again.

It's the Living that's Important, Not the Understanding

I would like to share with you my good friend Rod Walton's response to one of my on-line posts. His words are so insightful:

"Hi Richard, Thank you for sharing your journey with me and others, I have traveled the exact same journey as you, and have come to the same conclusions as you. Once the mist clears and you can see how simple and uncomplicated the message of Jesus was and is, all the theologies and dogma just seem irritating background music, and so much time and energy is wasted, instead of living the message of Jesus people argue over the message of Jesus. The Church ends up very much like the religious leaders of Jesus time, talking instead of doing. God bless."

Rod is absolutely right. It's the living of our lives that is important, not the understanding. My studies have answered some important questions for me and helped eliminate much of the fear associated with death. But in a sense, I have circumvented an obstacle that is actually supposed to be there. The fear of death, along with the not knowing, adds a sense of reality to the dream we call life. It creates a negative context of sorts for us in which to be brave and selfless. The negative aspects of life provide the opportunity for us to sacrifice for the benefit of others, which is the very essence of *agape* love. According to John 15:13, *"Greater love has no one than this: to lay down one's life for one's friends."* If we all viewed dying as a positive experience, then we would not have opportunity to express love in the way described in that verse. Yes, it stinks that people have to suffer and die. It stinks that life has to

163

be so hard. By contrast, however, once we die and leave these stinky lives of ours behind, what glory that will be!!!

But enough of death and dying. The Gospel of Christ is mainly for the living. Jesus came not only to teach us about life after death, He came to show us how to live abundantly. When we learn to express love and kindness in our life, in spite of our fears and not knowing how things might turn out, we create happiness for ourselves and others in the present moment, a kind of happiness that depends on nothing else. When we learn to love just for the sake of love itself we become happy.

What Is Meant by the Resurrection of the Body?

Have you ever thought of the physical resurrection of the body as a spiritual resurrection that only seems physical? Here's what I mean. Technically, from a quantum point of view, our physical bodies don't exist. All that actually exists, in the exact "current moment" in space/time, is a range of super-positioned quantum possibilities. Technically, the microscopic components of our physical bodies blink into and out of existence with each passing Planck unit of space/time. In other words, our bodies are not physical at all. When we are "resurrected" and given spiritual bodies in the heavenlies, our physical bodies are not resuscitated. They don't even exist. Even if you believe they exist in the present, they won't exist after they decay in the ground, and most certainly will not exist hundreds of years from now at some future supposed general resurrection date. Technically, there will be no physical bodies to resurrect.

So, what is the meaning of resurrection in the Bible? Well, on the surface it appears that the physical body is resuscitated, as with Lazarus and Jesus, as evidenced by the empty tomb and post-resurrection appearances. But what really happened? I don't believe that actual physical bodies were resurrected. Lazarus' body was changed. His old body disappeared and he was simultaneously given a new body to replace his old body. The new body he was given was suitable for life on earth, not heaven. Jesus' old body also disappeared, but he was given a spiritual body suitable for life in the heavenlies. It temporarily had the appearance of a physical body, and you could even touch and feel it, but that was only an illusion, as evidenced by the fact that Jesus could appear and disappear and even walk through walls.

Paul said, in 1 Cor. 15, our fleshly bodies (ie. flesh and blood) cannot inherit immortality. Instead we will be given new bodies, spiritual bodies suitable for life in heaven. So the only question remains, when does this happen, immediately upon death or at some future resurrection date? Since I believe we are basically spiritual, not physical beings, I believe this happens immediately upon death. If in fact it happens at a future date, it would certainly "seem" to us as though it were immediately upon death. Time is measured differently in the heavenlies than here on earth.

Here's a Real Mind-Bender for You.

According to some physicists, who are spiritually oriented and understand the true nature of reality, we are (present tense) spiritual beings who actually reside in an infinite realm outside of this finite space/time universe. We are viewing our earthly existence through the lens of our quasi-physical brains. According to the Bible, Christ is the "source" of us all. He is where we all originated. Through Him everything was created. *"In Him we live and move and have our being."* In a very real sense God the Father and Christ are one and the same. We are already "saved in Christ." The word "created" gives the false impression that we had a beginning in time, but time only exists, as we know it, within the confines of this space/time universe. We are actually eternal, infinite beings. Technically, we have always existed and always will exist.

It is only the space/time universe, and our experience within it, that had a beginning. Because it is finite, it will also have an end. After we depart from it, from our new vantage point, we will be able to revisit it any time we wish, as one revisits the past or relives a dream. We will be able to re-enter it and leave it as often as we wish. Nothing that happens in it will ever be lost. Every memory remains. No thought, word or deed will be forgotten. Even though it has already ceased to exist from a temporal standpoint, it will still exist in our thoughts and memories. Can you see how all this ties in with Scripture?

According to the Apostle Paul in 1 Corinthians 13, the only thing that lasts forever and will never pass away is love. That is the very definition of God the Father and Jesus Christ (our source). Love is not temporal. It is eternal. When you find yourself overwhelmed by the trials of this life, try to understand that when compared to eternity, this life has already passed, as in the blink of an eye. It's already over, except in your earthly conscious awareness. You are experiencing a vivid dream from which you will wake up in the arms of your loving heavenly Father (metaphorically speaking). Your Father is right here in the room with you. Anytime you wish, you can reach out and hold His hand. He is always watching over you. Nothing can separate you from His love.

1 Corinthians 13:8-*13* *"Love never ends. As for prophecies, they will pass away; as for tongues, they will cease; as for knowledge, it will pass away. For we know in part and we prophesy in part, but when the perfect comes, the partial will pass away. When I was a child, I spoke like a child, I thought like a child, I reasoned like a child. When I became a man, I gave up childish ways. For now we see in a mirror dimly, but then face to face. Now I know in part; then I shall know fully, even as I have been fully known. So now faith, hope, and love abide, these three; but the greatest of these is love."*

The Water Is Calm Beneath the Surface

Beneath the surface of a raging sea lie the calm waters of the deep. Some, perhaps most, Christians cannot see beneath the surface of Biblical literalism, and they get caught up in endless debate. Beneath the surface of Christian dogma, and the dogma of most other world religions as well, lies the beautiful and transformative truth that God is love. There is a loving purpose behind everything that God does, and our purpose in life is to become like Him.

We can argue all day about the deity of Christ and the existence of a place called Hell. We can argue about the post, mid, or pre-tribulation rapture. We can argue 'til the cows come home about pre, post and amilennialim, faith vs. works, whether the Bible is literally true or not, and so on. But the most important truth is so simple. God is love, and we need to be about the business of expressing the love of God in everything we say and do. If God is love, then the rest of our theology is only window dressing. If we get it wrong, our loving God will most certainly straighten us out when the timing is right. Sooner or later, we will all achieve theological correctness. The Spirit of God will lead all of us into the important truths.

When you find yourself getting all hot and bothered over superficial doctrinal issues, take a very deep breath, and dive deeply into the calming depths of God's love and remain there as long as you can. Let God worry about the turbulence on the surface. That's His problem, not yours. If you look up and see a desperate individual or loved one helplessly floundering on the surface above you, reach up and pull him or her into the place where you are. Hold that person in your calm, reassuring and loving arms.

Let us busy ourselves mostly with the doing of God's business, which is to express love, and not so much with the talking and arguing about it.

167

The Sick and Dying
Don't Need More Bad News.

Constructive criticism is most often viewed negatively, no matter how loving the intent. Its effect on people is often the opposite of what was intended. In the Bible we find many examples of people reacting negatively to the chastisements of God. They dig their feet in and continue to rebel. Many of the prophets were killed for their trouble. The judgments of God yield the *"peaceable fruit of righteousness,"* when directed at people whose hearts have been prepared by the Holy Spirit. Most often, however, the softening of the heart happens as a result of being shown mercy, rather than judgment. Sometimes people are so badly beaten down and so completely devoid of self-worth that constructive criticism only serves to pour salt on their wounds and makes them resist all the more.

The power of the Gospel of Christ is in the Cross. God's self-sacrificing love and forgiveness are very powerful motivators that can soften even the hardest of hearts. Being told that we are wrong is necessary for all of us, but we need to realize that the chastisements of God are primarily used to prepare our hearts to receive His love. They are not the end result, but instead are a necessary precursor to our receiving God's blessings. The Hells that we find ourselves in when we lose our way are used by God to humble us and break us free from our own stubborn self-will and prepare us to receive His love and forgiveness. God doesn't allow us to go through this just for the Hell of it. He does it for our good.

We need to realize that bad people don't need to be warned about Hell. They are already living in Hells of their own making. What they need are words of love and kindness. They need to know that God loves them, no matter what they have done. The Gospel of Christ is Good News, not bad news. The sick and dying don't need more bad news. What they need is healing.

God's Lost & Found

An important place in many institutions is the lost & found. At my granddaughter's school there is a "Lost & Found" room. In the Bible, the Greek word *"apollumi"* is translated *"lost,"* sometimes *"perished"* or *"destroyed."* In some cases the lost, perished or destroyed item or person is found, sometimes not. In the case of the "lost" coin, the "lost" sheep, or the "lost" Prodigal Son, that which was lost was found again. Sometimes it is used to describe the fate of unrighteous and wicked people, as in Romans 2:12, Peter 2:12, and 2 Thes. 2:9-10. The wicked and unrighteous are not forever lost. They are only lost until they are found again.

If you want to get technical about it, they have already been found but have not yet been redeemed and returned to their owner. They are in a manner of speaking in God's lost & found. They have been found and are just waiting to be picked up by their owner. They don't call the "lost & found" room at school the "lost" room. They call it the "lost & found" room because someone has already found the items in it. They are only being held there until their rightful owner comes to pick them up.

The Bible says that we are all like sheep, who have become lost (ie. perished). Jesus is our good shepherd and rightful owner, who came to earth to seek and save us. He is God incarnate, who, according to 1 Timothy 4:10, is the *"Savior of all men, and especially of those who believe."* He is already the Savior of all of us. Some of us have been returned to our owner, while others still remain in the lost & found room. God knows the precise location of all His lost sheep and has sent His Son to pick them up. Jesus said that after He goes back to Heaven He will prepare a place for us. When He is "lifted up" He will draw every last one of us back to our home in Heaven.

Does Satan Really Exist?

I don't believe that Satan is real. My view is that the writers of the Bible needed a way to explain the presence of evil in the world without blaming God, so an adversary, or Satan, was created (actually borrowed from the surrounding Babylonian culture). Much of the Old Testament was written and revised during the period of the Babylonian exile and soon afterwards. Jesus accommodated the popular beliefs in the Jewish culture. He may have believed that Satan was a separate entity. He was not omniscient.

In the various NDE (Near Death Experience) and OBE (Out of Body Experience) accounts, and from past-life and between-lives hypnotic regressions, we have learned that you are your own accuser. During the life review, your eyes are opened and you are able see your actions from a Godly perspective and from the perspective of people you may have harmed. But no one is judging you. You are at the same time experiencing unconditional love from God and from your friends in the spirit world. If Satan or evil spirits do exist, I seriously doubt they would be God's adversaries. In some way, they would, perhaps unwittingly, be serving the loving purposes of God. The experience of separation from God, and sin & evil in their various forms, are an important and necessary part of God's plan for all of us. They are necessary for our spiritual growth.

In some of the NDE's and OBE's we do see evidence, not of a single entity called Satan, but of evil spirits or entities. I am not at all sure that these entities have a real existence external to the experiencer's own "creative" thoughts. The effect is the same, however, whether they are real or just imagined. Are demons real external entities or just thought projections? I don't know. When Jesus cast out demons, the result was a freeing of the subject's mind from these negative influences. I believe that our entire human existence is a thought projection of sorts, an imagined reality created and shared by the collective consciousness of which we individually are tiny parts. Is Satan real? Only to the extent that we believe he is real. Is he able to negatively influence us? Only if we give him permission to do so.

What is a Christian?

Christianity may be defined in two ways. (1) It is the religion OF Jesus, and the man Jesus was/is our teacher and example, or (2) It is a religion ABOUT Jesus, whereby we worship Jesus as the unique Son of God.

The ancillary issue is this. How does one achieve salvation, however you might define it? Under scenario (1) we are saved by obeying Jesus and following His example. Under scenario (2) we are saved by believing about Jesus and acknowledging Him as Savior and Lord.

How does the love and grace of God fit into all of this? Under scenario (1) God is already our loving Father and we grow into relationship with Him by obeying the teachings of Jesus. Under scenario (2) God is already our loving Father but we cannot have a relationship with Him except through a belief in Jesus as our personal Lord and Savior.

Under scenario (1) we are saved by God the Father, with the man Jesus as our facilitator. Under scenario (2) we are saved by Jesus Christ, who is actually the same as God the Father, and eventually everyone will experience salvation, sooner or later.

My question for each of you is this. Does it really matter, which view you take? Under each scenario, God is at work in our lives before, during and after we learn about Jesus.

We Are Saved by Grace

When Paul says we are *"saved by grace"* and our salvation is *"not of ourselves"* and is a *"gift of God,"* I don't believe he is saying that we do not do anything at all, that we do not in any way "participate" in the salvation process. What He is saying is that we are carried along by the Holy Spirit who gives us the ability to do what we cannot do for ourselves. There is no room for boasting.

The Salvation "process" has two aspects to it. The first aspect has to do with God's forgiveness and complete acceptance of us as His beloved children, and raising us up from the dead and taking us back to our home in heaven when we die. For that to happen, we do absolutely nothing. When we die, all of us, without exception, are enlivened spiritually and given spiritual bodies and returned back to our source, our Heavenly Father in Heaven. This gift cannot be earned in any way.

The quality of our life, before and after death, however, is another matter, and that has to do with another very important aspect of our salvation experience, our being made into the likeness of Christ, or what you might call the "reformation of our character." Some theologians like to call it "sanctification." This is a process that we "work out" in relationship with God the Holy Spirit. This is what I referred to above as the being "carried along by the Holy Spirit." The Holy Spirit of God enables us to overcome the weakness of the flesh and become more like Christ during our earthly walk. The Spirit of God also helps us after death as we continue making even more progress. None of us enters the heavenly realms with fully-reformed characters. This second aspect of our salvation experience, the becoming like Christ, is an ages-long process. It does not culminate until the end of the ages.

What Should We Be Praying For?

I am here reminded of Martin Zender's hilarious story about two churches who were praying with cross purposes. One group was praying for rain, and the other was praying for good weather for their church picnic. God was in a quandary and didn't know what do to. I am also reminded of the example given by a quantum physicist that sometimes one person's intentions can be at cross purposes with another's. For example, if two individuals are approaching a traffic light from different directions, the light cannot turn green for both of them at the same time. I believe that there is a divine blueprint by which God governs the affairs of mankind. However, He allows us individual latitude as to how we fit ourselves into that overall plan. There are almost an infinite number of routes we can all take that eventually get us ALL to the same destination. We often get in each other's way. That is why, in John 5:14, we are reminded of the importance of asking in accordance with God's will. Even Jesus was compelled to defer to the will of God as He agonized in the Garden of Gethsemane.

It's probably a very good thing that we cannot see God's ideal blueprint for our lives. The route God has chosen for us is probably not the one we would choose. There is no easy route to our final destination. Jesus did say, after all, that the broad, easy way leads to destruction (ie. becoming lost). The way that leads to the eternal (age-abiding) life is not an easy one. In the words of Robert Frost, it is *"the road less travelled."* Every path we take will eventually get us to God's final destination, but the best way is the one that was first paved by Jesus Christ. I can assure you, it is not the easiest way.

I believe that God has given us internal spiritual resources that enable us to accomplish seemingly impossible goals. I believe that both Christians and non-Christians, even atheists, have this power within them. We all have a divine nature and we all have inborn creative abilities. For this reason, we do need to be careful what we pray for. Getting what we pray for might be totally at cross

173

purposes with God's best path for us. We need to ask God's Holy Spirit to guide our thoughts and help us to pray for the right things. As we pray, we need to remember that many of life's most important lessons cannot be learned if God gives us everything we want.

So is it proper to ask for good things? Jesus did say that God loves to *"give good things to His children."* Is it OK for us to ask for divine protection when embarking on a trip? Is it OK to ask for a better job, when so many in our society, and especially people in third-world countries, have no jobs at all? Is it OK to ask God to prosper us? Is it OK to ask God to relieve our pain and suffering? Of course it is, but at the same time we need know that there is a loving purpose behind every "no" answer. Whatever we ask, we need also to ask that God's will, not necessarily ours, be done.

If we do this, God will answer in one of four ways: (1) Yes, (2) No, (3) Wait a while, or (4) Roll up your sleeves and get to work.

The Greatest Commandment

How does one go about obeying the greatest commandment, that we love God with all of our heart, soul and mind? I have never been able to conjure up within myself what some would describe as a genuine love for God, at least not in the way that one would expect. Most people envision God as an invisible, male spirit being who lives somewhere up in Heaven and who looks in on us from time to time. Like most fathers, He loves us, but unlike most fathers, He never audibly speaks to us and is for all practical purposes absent from our lives. How does one go about loving a God like that? *Agape*, self-sacrificing love, the kind of love described in the Bible, is not easy to express towards an invisible spirit being who expects a lot, but needs nothing, from us.

In order to correctly understand what Jesus was getting at when He gave us the greatest commandment, we need to expand our concept of God and pay close attention to the corollary that Jesus gave to that commandment. He said the second commandment is like the first, that we love our neighbors as ourselves. What we fail to understand is the reason why the second commandment is like the first. It is not similar to the first because love is involved. It is similar because the object of our love is the same. Loving our neighbors is exactly the same as loving God

You can't have one without the other. If you claim to love God, without loving your neighbor, you are only fooling yourself. According to 1 John 4:20, *"Whoever claims to love God, yet hates a brother or sister, is a liar. For whoever does not love their brother and sister, whom they have seen, cannot love God, whom they have not seen."* That is why, in Matt. 25:40, Jesus said this to the surprised individual at the Kingdom gate, *"whatever you did for one of the least of these brothers and sisters of mine, you did for me."*

In order to fully understand why this is true, we need to expand our view of God. God is not just some disembodied spirit who lives in Heaven and occasionally swoops down over us to see what is going on, without directly interacting with us. God is infinitely bigger and greater than that. The broadest definition of God that I can think of is this. God is everything that is, and more. He exists both outside of and within all of creation, including each of us. We are all part of the divine Godhead because we were fashioned from God's own DNA, and God not only lives in each of us, He is each of us. We are each a tiny, but very important part of the Godhead. We are all God's children.

When I look at my children, and my children's children, I have a special affection for them because they are literally a part of me. They have developed separate egos or personalities, but they are part of me, nevertheless. Because we are manifestations of God, He is able to view the world through our very eyes, ears, feelings and emotions. Because He is at the same time greater than us, He is able to connect us with all other created beings.

So the conclusion of the matter is this, when we show love and compassion for ourselves and our neighbors, we are quite literally loving God.

The Cancellation of Our Sin Debt

If we confess our sins, he is faithful and just and will forgive us our sins and purify us from all unrighteousness. 1 John 1:9

God is love, and love "keeps no record of wrongs" (1 Cor. 13:5b). So, if God is not keeping score, why do we ask Him for forgiveness, each time we sin? Actually, I believe that many of us ask God for forgiveness for all the wrong reasons. Many of us don't fully understand what forgiveness and the love of God are really all about.

Have you ever asked yourself these questions: If our sins were covered by the blood of Christ on Calvary, why do we need to continually ask for forgiveness? Are Christians forgiven by God only for those past sins which are confessed? When we sin again, do we fall into an unforgiven state? Many Christians would argue that this is true and that it is possible to lose our salvation if we do not continually ask for forgiveness and if we do not persevere in the faith until the day we die.

The reason for this mistaken view of Christian salvation has to do with an incorrect definition of the word "forgiveness." Many would incorrectly define forgiveness as "a cessation of animosity towards the offender." Under this definition, the person seeking forgiveness would say that he/she is sorry and ask the offended party to no longer be angry at them. If the offended party accepts the request for forgiveness, then he/she would no longer harbor feelings of anger or hostility toward the offender. Under this scenario, the process of forgiveness is initiated by the offender. The problem with applying this definition to our relationship with God is that God has initiated the process, not us. God is not angry at sinners. He demonstrated this on Calvary. Jesus did not come into the world to condemn us; He came to save us.

The correct definition of forgiveness is letting someone know that you love them and are not mad at them and that you hold no animosity towards them. Under this scenario, the offender does not even have to ask for forgiveness. There is no need to ask.

Forgiveness can also be correctly defined as "cancelling a debt." However, in the case of our sin debt, we don't owe the debt to God. The sin debt might best be defined as an accumulation of necessary corrective chastisements that would be required to right the wrong or bring about a necessary reformation of character.

Why are we asked in 1 John 1:9 to confess our sins? We do it so that we might be *"purified from all unrighteousness."* If we don't confess and repent of our sins, we do suffer the chastisements of God, which mostly take the form of the natural earthy consequences of our actions. God does not chastise us because He is mad at us. He doesn't do it because He is offended by our actions. He doesn't do it to even the score. He does it because He loves us. He has always loved us.

In light of the above, I would offer this paraphrase of 1 John 1:9:

"If we confess our sins, He is faithful and just to remove the chastisement and help us to overcome the sin in our lives."

Christian salvation, I believe, is a process of experiencing in our human awareness something that has already happened from God's perspective. Asking God to forgive us does not change God in any way. We are the ones who are changed.

How to Experience a Personal Relationship with God

A few years ago, I read from a book of poems by one of my wife's ancestors, who was not a religious man. He said the best way to pray to God is with our actions. God does keep most of us in the dark with respect to the finer points of doctrine. But there is no mistaking the needs of those who need a helping hand. And there is no mistaking their gratitude when you lend a hand. And there is no mistaking the overwhelming sense of joy one experiences afterwards. Jesus mostly focused on the doing, not the theology or external religious observance. Religious ecstasy, or the joy that people find in a direct mystical relationship with the Spirit of God, has for the most part eluded me. But the joy that may be found in helping someone in need is readily available to anyone. When we love one another, we are loving God. When we are loved by another, God is expressing His love for us. We all possess the divine nature (ie. Christ within), and it is through human relationships that God personally relates to us.

The Fatherhood of God

I believe we are literally children of God, made from Christ's spiritual DNA. Jesus was "begotten" (ie. birthed) by the Father. By extension, we are all literally offspring of God the Father through Christ. If Christ created us, and Christ is God, then God created us. God has both paternal and maternal aspects to His character. If we were to take literally the fatherhood of God, without reference to His motherhood, how could God literally be our father? It is the mother, not the father, who actually gives birth. The mother is impregnated with the Father's seed, and that seed joins with the mother's to form a complete being.

So I believe that, in a sense, the term "our Father" is to some degree metaphorical and anthropomorphic. God does not have male body parts, or a long white beard, or arms, legs and feet. God

178

is not a physical being. He is spirit. If you want to be more accurate, you might want to refer to God as both our mother and father. God is not limited to the physical male gender. In saying that, I don't mean to minimize the "personhood" of God. On the contrary, God is more than a person. He is the sum of all the persons in the universe that He created, AND MORE.

Jesus lived in a highly patriarchal society. Referring to God as father/mother or just mother, would not have adequately described God's authority and sovereignty. Perhaps the ancient Hebrews had it right when they originally assigned to God an unpronounceable name. There are no words to describe what or who God is. He just is. All descriptions are imperfect. They can only describe some of God's attributes in human, anthropomorphic terms.

So, what did Jesus mean when He called God Father? I don't believe He was intending to limit His description to gender. He was referring mainly to the aspects of fatherhood which transcend the physical. We are literally God's offspring, emanating from God's own being. Jesus was also picturing, in human terms, the unconditional love that a Father has for His child, the kind of love that a human father cannot have for someone else's child.

THE END

Made in the USA
Monee, IL
06 November 2021

81192438R00104